SONGS TO LIVE BY

Studies in the Psalms and Christian Worship

By Ken Chant

SONGS TO LIVE BY

Studies in the Psalms and Christian Worship

By Ken Chant

ISBN 978-1-61529-085-7

Copyright © 2013 By Ken Chant

Vision Publishing
1672 Main St. E 109
Ramona, CA 92065
1-800-9-VISION
WWW.BOOKSBYVISION.COM

All rights reserved worldwide

No part of the book may be reproduced in any manner whatsoever without written permission of the author except in brief quotations embodied in critical articles of reviews.

A NOTE ON GENDER

It is unfortunate that the English language does not contain an adequate generic pronoun (especially in the singular number) that includes without bias both male and female. So *"he, him, his, man, mankind,"* with their plurals, must do the work for both sexes. Accordingly, wherever it is appropriate to do so in the following pages, please include the feminine gender in the masculine, and vice versa.

FOOTNOTES

A work once fully referenced will thereafter be noted either by "ibid" or "op. cit."

Note: the book of psalms is an integral part of this study. So as part of the course you should read right through the psalms at least once.

A companion book to this one "The Worship Leader" is attached to the end of this study. It is a practical manual of instruction on platform and music technique.

CONTENTS

A CURE FOR SNAKE BITE!	7
PART ONE: IN THE TEMPLE OF GOD	9
CHAPTER ONE MIRRORS OF THE SOUL	10
ADDENDUM FURTHER EXAMPLES OF ORACULAR PSALMS	27
CHAPTER TWO THE FIVE BOOKS	29
CHAPTER THREE A STUDY IN POETRY	39
CHAPTER FOUR A BEAUTY OF IDEAS	51
CHAPTER FIVE ANGRY PSALMS	65
CHAPTER SIX PILGRIMS AND PROPHECIES	73
PART TWO: AT THE THRONE OF GRACE	91
PREFACE THE WORSHIP LEADER	92
CHAPTER SEVEN PERSONAL MOTIVATION	95
CHAPTER EIGHT PROFESSIONALS APPROVED	109
CHAPTER NINE THE SOUND OF PROPHECY	121
ADDENDUM A THING OF BEAUTY	131
CHAPTER TEN PRINCIPLES OF WORSHIP	137
ADDENDUM ONE THE CHURCH FATHERS	145
ADDENDUM TWO APPLAUSE	155
ADDENDUM THREE SOME SCRAPS OF PERSONAL PREJUDICE	159
PART THREE: THE WORSHIP LEADER	163
CHAPTER ELEVEN LOOKING AT YOURSELF!	164
CHAPTER TWELVE PLATFORM TECHNIQUE	181
CHAPTER THIRTEEN MUSIC TECHNIQUE	195
CHAPTER FOURTEEN SONG TECHNIQUE	205

4

ABBREVIATIONS

Abbreviations commonly used for the books of the Bible are

Genesis	Ge	Habakkuk	Hb
Exodus	Ex	Zephaniah	Zp
Leviticus	Le	Haggai	Hg
Numbers	Nu	Zechariah	Zc
Deuteronomy	De	Malachi	Mal
Joshua	Js		
Judges	Jg		
Ruth	Ru	Matthew	Mt
1 Samuel	1 Sa	Mark	Mk
2 Samuel	2 Sa	Luke	Lu
1 Kings	1 Kg	John	Jn
2 Kings	2 Kg	Acts	Ac
1 Chronicles	1 Ch	Romans	Ro
2 Chronicles	2 Ch	1 Corinthians	1 Co
Ezra	Ezr	2 Corinthians	2 Co
Nehemiah	Ne	Galatians	Ga
Esther	Es	Ephesians	Ep
Job	Jb	Philippians	Ph
Psalm	Ps	Colossians	Cl
Proverbs	Pr	1 Thessalonians	1 Th
Ecclesiastes	Ec	2 Thessalonians	2 Th
Song of Songs	Ca *	1 Timothy	1 Ti
Isaiah	Is	2 Timothy	2 Ti
Jeremiah	Je	Titus	Tit
Lamentations	La	Philemon	Phm
Ezekiel	Ez	Hebrews	He
Daniel	Da	James	Ja
Hosea	Ho	1 Peter	1 Pe
Joel	Jl	2 Peter	2 Pe
Amos	Am	1 John	1 Jn
Obadiah	Ob	2 John	2 Jn
Jonah	Jo	3 John	3 Jn
Micah	Mi	Jude	Ju
Nahum	Na	Revelation	Re

Ca is an abbreviation of *Canticles,* a derivative of the Latin name of the *Song of Solomon*, which is sometimes also called the *Song of Songs.*
<u>Note</u>: scripture translations are my own unless otherwise noted.

A CURE FOR SNAKE BITE!

> Let God arise!
> Let his enemies be scattered!
> Let all who hate him flee from him in terror!
> Drive them away like smoke before a wind;
> Melt them like wax in a hot flame;
> So will the wicked perish in the presence of God!

Few today would hazard their lives on such a superstitious belief, but we can trust without any qualm the power of the *Psalms* to rescue us from the far greater venom of that old viper Satan. Here, in Israel's sacred songs, is a divine antivenene for all of the Serpent's poison. Those who read the *Psalms,* and reflect upon them continually, will surely find their promise fulfilled –

> Happiness belongs to everyone
> Whose delight is in the law of the Lord,
> Who meditate in his law day and night.
> They will be like trees planted beside a running stream,
> Which bear much fruit year after year
> And their leaves never wither (1:1-3)

These are truly "[1]songs to live by", and I hope that the following pages will quicken in you a new interest in the *Psalms,* and a desire to know much more about them. The first part of this book deals with the psalmody of Israel, and the second half builds on Israel's worship experience and explores some aspects of worship in the church.

Let me now launch the book with some lines by *Sir* Thomas Wyatt, that renowned English courtier and poet who nearly lost his head (literally) for love, when he sought to displace King Henry VIII in Anne Boleyn's affections. One of his poems is a song of eight stanzas, of which I shall quote the first here, and the last at the end of this book. A song about a man who was about to write a song seems appropriate to my theme!

My lute *awake!* perform the last
Labour that thou and I shall waste,
And end that I have now begun:
And when this song is sung and past,
My lute be still, for I have done.

Part One

IN THE TEMPLE OF GOD

Chapter One

MIRRORS OF THE SOUL

INTRODUCTION

Martin Luther described the Book of Psalms as *"a Bible in miniature;"* and it is indeed true that for nearly 20 centuries Christians of all churches have found the Psalter to be *"a Bible within the Bible."* No other Old Testament book speaks so warmly to the heart and soul of Christians. It is not unusual to find the New Testament printed with the *Book of Psalms*; but how often have you seen *"The New Testament and Isaiah"*, or *"The New Testament and Genesis"*?

The Psalms are passionate outpourings of the human soul. They mirror the full range of human emotions - from deepest despair to heights of ecstasy. They reflect virtually every life-situation, every spiritual problem, every yearning that the people of God experience as they journey from earth to heaven.

The Psalms also dispel pious pretense in prayer. They teach us to approach God honestly, stripped of every hypocritical facade. The Psalter abounds with complaints against, as well as praise for, God and his providence. The psalmists said what they felt, and spoke what they meant. They did not pretend to be something they were not. But that same naked honesty also compelled them to see God clearly, and thus finally return to an affirmation of faith (cp. Ps 44:8-12,17-19,23-26.)

Hardly anything could more enrich your life than to become familiar with these glorious and profoundly moving songs.

GENERAL INFORMATION

♦ THE PSALMS AND PUBLIC WORSHIP

In Hebrew, the title of the collection is *tehillim* = *"Songs of Praise."* Why then do we call them *"psalms"*? Simply because our English words *Psalms* and *Psalter* are derived from the Latin *psalmorum* and the Greek *psalterion*.

Those words were themselves both derived from an older word that meant to *twang* or *pluck;* hence they described a song accompanied by a harp or some other stringed instrument. Thus we are reminded that the Psalms are poems designed more to be sung than read; they are not formal sermons nor doctrinal statements.

Is that important?

Yes, because it means that they cannot be properly understood unless they are read as you would read any other song. How do you read a song? Certainly not in the same way you would read a piece of prose. Readers of poetry adopt (usually unconsciously) a particular emotional, spiritual, and mental attitude. They expect the real meaning of the lines to lie under the surface. They look for the words to appeal to the heart rather than to the mind.

Further, poets and songwriters often talk about one thing when they mean the reader to understand another. They use a figure of speech called a "conceit", in which ideas that seem to have no connection are used to represent each other. For example, consider these two English poems, both of which employ clever devices that have nothing to do with their actual theme:

- Shakespeare, in one of his sonnets, uses the image of a weary traveler to express his love for his sweetheart; he yearns for her as a man would who was obliged to journey far from his home and his beloved -

    How heavy do I journey on the way,

    When what I seek - my weary travel's end -

    Doth teach that ease and that repose to say,

    'Thus far the miles are measur'd from thy friend!'[1]

    The beast that bears me, tired with my woe,

---

[1] **Lines 1-4**. When he gets to the end of his journey, and should find rest, he will instead be reminded how far distant he is from his beloved.

Plods dully on, to bear that weight in me,

As if by some instinct the wretch did know

His rider lov'd not speed, being made from thee:[2]

The bloody spur cannot provoke him on

That sometimes anger thrusts into his hide;

Which heavily he answers with a groan,

More sharp to me than spurring to his side;[3]

For that same groan doth put this in my mind -

My grief lies onward, and my joy behind.[4]

— John Donne, in A Hymn to Christ (written in 1619), uses the analogy of a sea voyage to express his faith in the Saviour —

In what torn ship soever I embark,[5]

That ship shall be my emblem of thy ark;

What sea soever swallow me, that flood

Shall be to me an emblem of thy blood;[6]

---

[2] <u>Lines 5-8</u>. His sorrow is so heavy that even the animal feels its extra weight

[3] So burdensome is the load, not even the spur can hasten the beast, but its groan of pain reminds the rider of his own hurt.

[4] The entire journey, of course, is imaginary; the poet is simply employing the "conceit" of a journey as a device to express how greatly he loves his sweetheart.

[5] As it happens, Donne actually did undertake a dangerous sea journey in the English diplomatic service; but he still turns it into a poetic "conceit, as a vehicle to express his trust in God.

[6] <u>Lines 1-4</u>. He resolves that every aspect of the voyage will be used to remind him of God's mercy and salvation.

> Though thou with clouds of anger do disguise
> Thy face; yet through that mask I know those eyes,
> Which, though they turn away sometimes,
> They never will despise.[7]
>
> I sacrifice this Island unto thee,
> And all whom I loved there, and who loved me;[8]
> When I have put our seas 'twixt them and me,
> Put thou thy sea betwixt my sins and thee.[9]
> As the tree's sap doth seek the root below
> In winter, in my winter now I go,
> Where none but thee, th'eternal root
> Of true love I may know.[10]

How nonsensical it would be for someone to use either of those poems as a source of teaching about (say) the rigors of travelling by mule-back, or about the perils of an ocean voyage! Yet just that kind of folly can often be observed in interpretations of the Psalms. The lesson is clear: *poetry* must be read and understood as *poetry,* not as formal prose, whether it is found in a set of love sonnets, or in a hymn book, or in the Bible.

How to read the Psalms will become more evident later, as we study the peculiar structures of Hebrew poetry. But here let us notice that the Psalter is

---

[7] <u>Lines 5-8.</u> He is learning never to doubt that God loves him, no matter how terrifying the circumstances, or how hidden the face of God may seem

[8] England is farewelled.

[9] <u>Lines 3, 4</u> As the sea will separate him from his home, so may the grace of God remove him from his sin

[10] <u>Lines 5-8</u>. He will use the coming perils to force him deeper into faith

actually a hymn book, designed for use in Israel's worship, and showing the liturgical[11] structure of the Temple services. We learn that Israel's worship was highly formal, yet also warmly spontaneous -

> "The Psalter is Israel's hymn book ... Many of the Psalms carry musical or liturgical directions. The text of some refers to a public liturgy - 20, 26, 27, 66, 81, 107, 116, 134, 135. These last, and others - 48, 65, 95, 96, 118 - were evidently recited in the Temple court. The Songs of Ascents (120 - 134), like 84, were songs used on the Temple pilgrimage. These are some of the clearest examples, and suffice to show that many Psalms, even individual Psalms, were composed for Temple worship. Others, if not composed primarily for this purpose, have at least been adapted for it by the addition of blessings - 125, 128, 129 ... It is therefore certain that the Psalms were related to public worship and that the Psalter, taken as a whole, is liturgical in character ... (Thus) the Hebrew title of 92 assigns it to the Sabbath day, and the Greek titles of 24, 48, 93, 94 apportion them to several other days of the week ... "[12]

Clearly then, the Psalms were either composed or adapted for use in the worship services of the Temple, and served much the same purpose as hymn books do in Christian churches.

The structure of many of the Psalms reflects this liturgical use. With a little imagination, and an expansion of some of the Psalms, it is easy to feel that one has been carried back across the centuries into the Temple, to share in one of Israel's days of public assembly. Here we are, standing with the great

---

[11] The word "Liturgy" means simply an "order of service", especially one that is fixed in some way, ether by being written down, or by its long usage. Consciously, or unconsciously all churches, (even Pentecostal groups) develop a worship liturgy – that is a common or habitual sequence of song, prayer, reading, praise, oblations, preaching, eucharistic observance and the like.

[12] From the New Jerusalem Bible, "Introduction to the Psalms", section Five.

congregation, worshipping Yahweh in the courts of his magnificent sanctuary in old Jerusalem. We can do this, because many of the liturgical Psalms seem to represent a poet's summary, or description, of a striking worship service that he had experienced. The psalmist was so moved by the service that he determined to commemorate it forever in a song. Later, his poem was added to Israel's Psalter, and then itself became a part of other liturgies. We will explore more of that process in a moment. But first note that observation of the liturgical structure of the Psalms helps to explain a mystery: why do so many of these sacred songs have such an irregular pattern? The constantly changing poetical structure of many Psalms reflects the place each new section had in the liturgy. Or perhaps the abrupt changes in mood or speaker show a shift in the action or ritual of the worship service.

One group of Psalms is particularly interesting, namely, the collection of songs that embody a prophetic oracle. They convey a strong impression that from time to time a prophet spontaneously disturbed the orderly progression of the liturgy or priest, who suddenly spoke out a word from the Lord. These disrupted Psalms show the charismatic nature of Israel's worship, and suggest that a devout worshipper from ancient Israel would feel quite at home in a modern Pentecostal environment!

Here then are some examples of

♦ LITURGICAL PSALMS WITH ORACLES

In each of the examples below you should imagine yourself peacefully sharing in the stately ritual of the Temple, when suddenly the voice of a prophet cries out. The word of the Lord interrupts the ceremony, and reshapes the worship of the people. Everybody is stirred; the planned program is perhaps abandoned. Depending upon the nature of the oracle, sounds of lamentation or of joy echo through the sanctuary. God has spoken, and the people must respond. Sometime later, the memorable event was summarised by the psalmist in a poem. He hoped the worshippers would never forget that day!

How can you recognise these special Psalms? As you will see from the following the occurrence of an oracle in the Psalms may be marked by various signals:

- perhaps there is a change of speaker - say, from the psalmist to the Lord, then back to the psalmist;[13] or
- sometimes, the intrusion of an oracle is shown by an expression such as, *"The Lord speaks in his sanctuary ... "* or, *"This is what God says ... "*
- or there may be just a dramatic change in the direction, theme, or mood of a Psalm.

Here are some examples -

Psalm 12, a lament, seeking deliverance from personal enemies.

- a cry for help, perhaps uttered by a worshipper, or by the Temple cantor, to introduce the time of worship;
- (5) the Lord's response, through a sudden prophetic oracle, promising protection for those who call upon him;
- an affirmation of faith, perhaps by the cantor, or another official, encouraging the people to rely upon the oracle;
- an anthem by the choir, responding to the oracle and praying for the promise to be soon fulfilled.

Psalm 20, a liturgy for a sacrifice offered before a battle.

- a prayer sung while approaching the altar, seeking the blessing of God upon their sacrifices (vs. 3), and pleading that the army might be given victory in the coming battle (vs. 4-5);
- a joyful response by a prominent person to an oracle [14] that was presumably spoken between verses 5 & 6 (for a similar

---

[13] For example, Psalm 91:1-13, which reads like a summary of a sermon, which was then either interrupted by, or climaxed by, an oracle, delivered as if God were the speaker. (vs 14-16).

[14] Note the use of the singular pronoun "I". The person referred to may have been either the worship leader, a priest, the king or perhaps the psalmist himself.

hiatus, see 28:5-6; 69:29-30, and compare the placing of the oracle in *Psalm 21* below);[15]

- (7-8) a worship leader gives a more formal response to the oracle, or perhaps simply resumes the original liturgy

- (9) the choir, or perhaps the people or the army, sing a closing anthem.[16]

Psalm 21, a liturgy for thanksgiving after victory in battle.

- (1-7) God is praised (perhaps by the king himself, acting as worship leader in a regal liturgy) for the victory he has given to Israel;

- (8-12) a prophet interrupts the king with an oracle promising yet greater victories;

- (13) the congregation, or perhaps the army, sings the praises of God.

Psalm 50, a Psalm built around two oracles.

- an introduction to the two oracles that follow (note the opening words: *"God, the Lord God, has <u>spoken</u>"*), which were perhaps spoken at different times, but so impressed the psalmist that he (or she) copied them down and then wrought them into this *Psalm* -

- (7) the first oracle, beginning with an announcement that God is about to speak

- (8-15) a protest against violations of religious forms

---

[15] The oracle itself is of course now lost. (perhaps because of the inadvertent error of and ancient copyist); but its existence can be inferred from the dramatic change in mood and sentiment that occurs with verse 6. Apart from the reference cited above, other examples of this phenomenon can be found in the Psalms.

[16] Note the change of the pronoun to the plural "we".

- (16a) the second oracle, again beginning with an announcement
- (16b-23) the second oracle, denouncing violations of moral law.

Psalm 60, a liturgy following defeat in battle.
- (1-3) the people lament the defeat of their army in battle;
- an official prays that God might enable the king ("Thy Beloved") to regather the forces of Israel and to triumph over his enemies;
- the voice of a prophet suddenly echoes through the sanctuary with a jubilant oracle;
- (9-11) a general, or the king, responds to the oracle with a prayer;
- (12) the people, or the army, declare their renewed confidence in God.

Psalm 75, a liturgy of thanksgiving for God's mighty deeds.
- the choir sings the praises of God, and calls the people to worship;
- (2-5) the service is interrupted by a sudden oracle, spoken by a priest or prophet;
- (6-7) a warning based on the oracle, perhaps spoken by a priest or preacher;
- (8) a short poem on divine judgment, possibly sung by the choir, which may mark a return to the original order of service;
- an individual, probably the king, praises God and affirms confidence in the divine promise.

Psalm 81, a liturgy for a Temple festival.
- (1-5a) the call to worship;
- (5b) a priest or prophet suddenly senses the voice of God (*"I hear a voice I was not expecting ... "*);

- <u>the oracle is spoken</u>, and apparently had such an effect that it terminated the liturgy, since nothing else was spoken.

Psalm 82, a liturgy of judgment upon false judges.
- a seer declares his vision;
- (2-4) an oracle rebuking the false judges;
- (5) a teacher comments on the oracle;
- (6-7) <u>a second oracle, pronouncing sentence upon the false judges</u>; followed by (8) a prayer that the vision will be fully accomplished.

Psalm 85, a liturgy for deliverance from adversity.
- (1-3) God's past favours are retold;
- (4-7) a prayer for his favour to be restored;
- (8) a prophet waits for the Lord to speak (*"I will listen for God's reply ..."*);
- the oracle comes to him, and he declares it to the people, at which point the liturgy apparently came to an end.

Psalm 95, a liturgy for public worship.
- (1-2) the call to begin worship by singing a hymn;
- (3-5) the priest or cantor declares the greatness of God;
- (6-7a) the people are called to prayer;
- (7b-11) <u>a passionate oracle is suddenly delivered</u>, which is quite out of character with the happy beginning of the Psalm; it shattered the serene progress of the order of service, interjected the mind of God, and apparently terminated the planned liturgy for that day.

Other examples of prophetic oracles occurring at various points in the temple services - sometimes sought for by the worship leaders, sometimes unsought - could be readily found.[17] If you let your imagination carry you back to the Temple as you read the Psalms, you can get an exciting sense of the immediacy of God's presence and action among his people. Truly, as one of the Psalms says, the Lord himself stood *"in the midst of the great congregation"* (22:22; cp. He 2:12).

NATURE AND STRUCTURE

♦ THE BEATING HEART OF SCRIPTURE

The Psalter is the second of 5 books that are mainly poetry: *Job, Psalms, Proverbs, Ecclesiastes, Song of Songs*. Poetry is found elsewhere in the OT (notably in the writings of the prophets - see below), but these five are recognised as being distinctly poetical in form. Standing at the heart of the OT, they are preceded by 17 books of history, and followed by 17 books of prophecy.

Can we see a parable of life in the central position of poetry in the Bible, and in the fact that so much of the Bible is shaped as poetry? When you meet harsh, dogmatic people, inflexible and hard in their attitudes, void of tenderness, you can probably assume (among other things) that they don't read any poetry. There is something about poetry that makes one more human, more in tune with the mystery of life. Some things can be said poetically that cannot be so well expressed in any other way. Elizabeth Barrett Browning (1806-61) described it as a disclosure of the "heart within blood-tinctured, of a veined humanity" -

> There, obedient to her praying, did I read aloud the poems
>
> Made to Tuscan flutes, or instruments more various of our own;
>
> Read the pastoral parts of Spenser - or the subtle interflowings

---

[17] For some more examples, see the Addendum at the end of this chapter.

> Found in Petrarch's sonnets - here's the book - the leaf is folded down!
>
> Or at times a modern volume - Wordsworth's solemn-thoughted idyll,
>
> Or from Browning[18] some "Pomegranate", which if cut deep down the middle,
>
> Shows a heart within blood-tinctured, of a veined humanity.[19]

So it is not an accident that a large body of poetry fills the central part of the Hebrew scriptures, with seventeen books of history on one side, and seventeen books of prophecy on the other. This layout suggests that if one knows only history and theology, then one's life and ministry will be incomplete. I think that every pastor and preacher should read poetry - not just the Psalms, but a wide range of poetry. It would imbue them with a deeper sensitivity to the human condition, it would save them from numerous follies I have observed over the years, it would immeasurably enrich their lives.

> "People who do not acquire and keep bright the love of poetry draw far less joy from life than those who do. Joseph Conrad once said that many travellers come back from their journeys having gained little more than the labels on their suitcases. Such, for all too many people, is the journey through life. They go here, they do this and that, but none of it leaves much impression. But to the mind nurtured on poetry, life becomes more significant, recollections of beautiful things become sharper, experience becomes deeper and wider. Poetry helps to create a keen awareness of life."[20]

---

[18] She is referring to her husband, the poet Robert Browning.

[19] From Lady Geraldine's Courtship

[20] Childrens Encyclopedia, ed. Arthur Mee; Educational Book society, London, 1963; Vol 1B, pg. 601.

♦ THE UNIQUENESS OF ISRAEL'S SONGS

- The Hebrews stand alone in their poetry. They are the only people whose entire extant poetry is directly or indirectly religious in content and purpose. Indeed, some have thought that Israel may never have produced any other kind of verse; but that seems unlikely, especially when the Song of Solomon is considered. The Song is a dramatic oratorio, which uses a choir and soloists to tell the story of a young man wooing and winning his bride; it celebrates the joy of human sexuality, and was presumably written for public performance. Notice also the lack of any religious content in David's great lyrical dirge over Saul and Jonathan (2 Sa 1:19-27).

  Nonetheless, although the Hebrews plainly did write non-religious poetry, it does seem that the Lord permitted the survival only of those writings that fitted his special task for Israel to be a light to the whole world (cp. Ro 3:1-2).

- The Psalter is not a complete collection of the songs of Israel; other examples of psalmody are scattered throughout the OT - for example, see 1 Sa 2:1-10; 2 Sa 1:17-27; Ne 9:5-37 (in some translations this is put as prose, not poetry). Nor did the writing of Psalms begin with David, as is often thought. They were a continuous part of Israel's worship from the most ancient times (see Ex 15:1-18; De 32:1-43; Jg 5:1-31; etc), and their composition was spread over at least a thousand years (from Moses to Malachi).

  Think about that in relation to English poetry, and how much our poetry has changed since (say) the year 1400 A.D.[21] and

---

[21] For example, here are a few lines from the "Prologue" of Geoffrey Chaucer's Canterbury Tales, written about 1387, describing a devout Oxford Scholar –

> For hym was levere have at his beddes heed
> Twenty bookes, clad in blak or reed,
> Of Aristotle and his philosophie,

Continued on next page

then note the remarkable similarity between the prayer of Moses (Ps 90), and the songs of David, 500 years later. We see here a mark of the divine superintendence over Israel's writings.

– But that brings us to another striking fact: Israel's songs were not peculiar to that nation. Modern readers are often astonished to discover that the Psalms emulate the style, contents, and structure, of hymns and prayers that were widely used in the ancient world. Israel's neighbours would not have found much that was unfamiliar in her national psalmody. Yet there was one significant difference. Hebrew poetry reflects a special genius, an awareness of the real nature of God and man, that is unique; it reaches heights of exaltation never attained by any other sacred songs; it exposes the inner life of the soul in a way that is unmatched by any other national literature.

The following selections show both those similarities and dissimilarities -

AN EGYPTIAN HYMN

How marvellous and varied are all the works that you have made!

No man can understand your mysteries,

O sole God, like whom there is no other!

According to your own purpose you have made the world,

By your own hand alone,

Than robes riche, or fithele, or sautrie,

But ak e that he was a philosphre,

Ye hadde he but litle gold in cofre.

("Levere" = rather; "Heed" = head; "reed"= red; "fithele" = fiddle; "sautrie" = psaltery [a stringed instrument].)

All people, the cattle, and the wild animals,

Whatever is on earth, walking upon its feet,

And what is in the sky, flying with its wings ...

You put every man in his right place,

You supply the needs of all people;

Everyone has his food,

And you have appointed the time of each person's end ...[22]

AN AKKADIAN HYMN

Worship the goddess, the most terrible of goddesses.

Let all fall down before the mistress of the peoples ...

Praise Ishtar, the most terrible of goddesses ...

She is garlanded with joyous beauty and love.

She is overflowing with alluring charm and sensuality;

Her mouth is full of sweetness; she speaks the word of life ...

She is the true goddess - wisdom is her possession,

And the destiny of all things lies in her grasp.

One look from her brings boundless joy;

Strength, honour, heaven's protection, undying vigilance (are found only in her).

Is there anyone who can equal her glory?

---

[22] From the pharaoh Akh-en-aton's Hymn to the Sun God, Egypt, 14th cent BC. As has been often remarked, it bears a striking resemblance to Ps 104:24-27, which was composed several hundred years later, although the psalmist could have had no knowledge of the pharaoh's poem.

All her commands are powerful; her words are highly exalted;

Ishtar! Before her majesty none can stand an equal![23]

A BABYLONIAN HYMN

You are mighty, O Lord, renowned among the nations,

You are the possessor of all knowledge.

How great is your splendour and perfection, O God, for are you not the Eternal One who can never die?

Your eye keeps watch over all men,

Your ear listens to their petitions,

You pour out upon them boundless blessing,

That is why all the people raise their prayer to you ...

O Lord, none other in heaven possesses your wisdom;

Open your mouth and command blessing upon me.

O Nabu, your understanding surpasses that of all gods;

Open your mouth and pronounce upon me endless life.

Are you not the light of all heaven and earth?

Your radiant glory embraces every nation.

From among the gods, I have sought only you,

And to you alone I offer my supplications.

I behold on your right hand justice, and on your left hand mercy;

The crown upon your head is kindness, grace, and peace;

Surrounding you there is only life and prosperity.[24]

---

[23] Based on an Akkadian Hymn to the goddess Ishtar, c. 1600 BC.

The general structure of those pagan Psalms, and the sentiments expressed in them, reflects a pattern that was common in the ancient world and that was largely copied by Israel. But out of that comes an arresting thought: if Israel's worship *structure* was so much like that of her neighbours, how is it that her spiritual *ethic* was so much higher?

It would be reasonable to expect that when the *outward* and practical aspects of Israel's civic, commercial, cultural, and religious life were basically the same as that of her contemporaries, then her *inner* and moral life would also be identical. As I have said already, Babylonians, Assyrians, Persians, Philistines, Arameans, visiting Israel's cities, even looking at her great temple in Jerusalem, would not have observed anything very different from the familiar scenes of their homelands; yet astonishment gripped them when they wanted to see Israel's God, for of him there was no image!

Yet we know that Israel would gladly have copied the heathen in *every* respect, for that is shown clearly enough by her constant tendency to adopt the practice of idolatry. But in the end she remained a nation apart, and we are left wondering why?

Even more startling was Israel's moral law, the lofty ethical principles enshrined in her statutes, the total absence of sensuality, of religious harlotry, from her observances. Again we are constrained to ask why?[25]

No other explanation save the one the Bible gives is adequate to explain this striking difference among so much resemblance: God was at work in Israel, giving to her laws, her worship, her sacred songs, a quality and nobility that was unique to that nation.

---

[24] From a Babylonian hymn, dated around 1750 BC

[25] Note again the reference to Ishtar's sensuality in the Akkadian hymn above. It was standard practice for centuries, of course, to have both male and female prostitutes attached to temples throughout the ancient world, including the later temples of Greece and Rome. The use of those prostitutes was an integral part of the worship of the deities honoured in each temple.

Addendum

FURTHER EXAMPLES OF ORACULAR PSALMS

1) **Psalm 28**: an oracle was probably spoken between verses 5 & 6.
2) **Psalm 30:** an oracle was probably spoken between verses 10 & 11.
3) **Psalm 31**: the abrupt transition between verses 18 & 19 suggest that an oracle was spoken, assuring the psalmist that his prayer had been heard by God.
4) **Psalm 32**: verses 8 & 9 are an oracle.
5) **Psalm 46**: verse 10 is an oracle.
6) **Psalm 55**: in verses 1-21 the poet addresses God; then there is a sudden change in verse 22 (an oracle), to which the poet responds in verse 23.
7) **Psalm 62**: this Psalm seems to be written in response to the two oracles in verses 11 ("Power belongs to God") and 12 ("Your love, O Lord, never fails.")
8) **Psalm 68**: verse 22 is an oracle.
9) **Psalm 73**: an oracle may have been spoken between verses 17 & 18.
10) **Psalm 87**: verse 4 is an oracle.
11) **Psalm 89**: there is an oracle in verses 3 & 4, with perhaps another in verses 19-37.
12) **Psalm 91**: verses 14-16 are an oracle.
13) **Psalm 102**: verses 18-20 may be a response to and a summary of an oracle.
14) **Psalm 108**: verses 7-9 are an oracle.

15) **Psalm 109**: an oracle may have been spoken between verses 29 & 30.

16) **Psalm 110**: contains several oracles spoken to the king.

From time to time as I am reading the Psalms I notice other examples, particularly of an apparent lacuna, where it seems that the psalmist is responding to an unrecorded oracle. But the above list is sufficient for the purpose of these notes. If you discover other occurrences of oracles, you could add them yourself to the list.

Chapter Two

THE FIVE BOOKS

The four most famous notes in music are probably the "hammer blows" that begin Beethoven's Fifth Symphony. Listening to them on one occasion, Beethoven himself said, "Thus fate knocks at the door!". At a performance of the symphony in Paris, a famous opera singer, Marie Malibran (1808-36), hearing the symphony for the first time, was so overwhelmed that she had an attack of the convulsions and had to be carried out of the concert hall! The great French Romantic composer Berlioz reckoned that those four opening notes revealed "Beethoven's most private grief's, his fiercest wrath, his most lonely and desolate meditations, his midnight visions, his bursts of enthusiasm."

We might say the same, and with more truth, about the *Book of Psalms*. They throb with passion, they resound with joy, they ache with love, they soar with praise, they tremble with grief, they echo with laughter!

When were *Psalms* first composed in Israel? They did not begin with David, as many suppose, although from his time on the art certainly flourished more richly. His name became so closely linked with Israel's songs and liturgy that the whole corpus was sometimes grouped under it. David's special contribution to the creation of Israel's psalmody is shown in scripture:

- he was a musician and composer (1 Sa 16-16-18; Am 6:5)
- he gave new form to Israel's liturgy (2 Sa 6:5,16; 1 Ch 15:16-28; 16:4-7,37-42; 25:1-8; 2 Ch 7:6; 29:30)
- he is called "the sweet psalmist of Israel" (2 Sa 23:1-2).

Several authors are given for the Psalms, and prior to the Exile various collections of Psalms (as we shall see below) came into existence. The authors are -

David	73 Psalms
Asaph	(12)Psalms 50, 73-83
The Sons of Korah	(12)Psalms 42-49, 84, 85, 87, 88
Solomon	(2)Psalms 72, 127
Heman	Psalm 88
Ethan	Psalm 89
Moses	Psalm 90, and perhaps also 91

while 50 of the Psalms are anonymous.

However, that list is based on the inscriptions to the Psalms, and concerning those there is some uncertainty. Notice the following -

- In many cases where the author of a Psalm is apparently mentioned, there is an ambiguity in the text

    the Hebrew word translated *"of"* may also mean *"to"* or *"for"* - hence it is uncertain, for example, whether the inscription to *Psalm 72* means *"by"* Solomon, or *"for"* Solomon

    see also the inscription to *Psalm 88*, which I have listed in Lesson One as being composed both by Heman and the Sons of Korah - in fact, the actual composer may have been someone else.

- All except 34 of the Psalms have Hebrew titles. The origin of those titles is unknown, but they were probably added to the Psalms by some person, or persons, other than the original authors. There are perhaps a few exceptions (such as Psalm 51) where the inscription describes the circumstances behind the writing of the Psalm, and may have been added to the Psalm by its author.

- The inscriptions describe either the reputed author of the Psalm, the time of its writing, the event that inspired it, the purpose for which it was written, the person to whom it was dedicated, or musical directions for its performance, and the type of song.

All those factors can be seen in the inscription to *Psalm 60*:

<u>Author</u>	probably David
<u>Time</u>	the occasion of David's conflict with Aram

Event	Joab's return with the army from Edom
Purpose	for instruction
Dedication	to the choirmaster
Directions	according to Shushan Eduth
Type	a Miktam.

- Some scholars reject the inscriptions altogether, claiming they are unreliable, and they are sometimes omitted from printed Bibles. However, they are of great antiquity, for they are known to have been part of the Psalter well before 300 B.C. A further mark of their age is the occurrence of several words that had become obsolete, and their meaning uncertain, by the 4th century B.C.; hence they were left untranslated, as they still are in many modern translations (scholars can only guess at their original meaning).

- It seems that the best approach to the inscriptions would be to treat them with respect, to refer to them as a guide to understanding the Psalms they head, but to use them with caution.

THE STRUCTURE OF THE PSALTER

◆ **THE FIVE BOOKS**

- The Psalter was very early divided by the Jews into Five Books, possibly as an attempt by an ancient editor (perhaps Ezra or Nehemiah) to imitate the Pentateuch. Thus the 5 books of the Law (the Torah) given by God to man are balanced by the 5 books of Prayer (the Psalms) given by man to God.

- The 5 sections are easily recognised by the doxology that brings each of them to a close, and in many Bibles each group is preceded by a heading, such as First Book. The Five Books of the Psalms are -

Book One............. Psalms 1-41 ....(doxology at 41:13)

Book Two .... Psalms 42-72 ....(doxology at 72:18-19, and note verse 20)

Book Three .... Psalms 73-89 ....(doxology at 89:52)

Book Four .... Psalms 90-106 .... (doxology at 106:48)

Book Five .... Psalms 107-150 .... (doxology, the whole Psalm)

- Note that those doxologies are not an original part of the Psalms to which they are now attached. Strictly speaking, therefore, they should be excluded from the interpretation of those Psalms, although most readers and commentators treat them as if each one does belong to the song it follows.

- Various attempts have been made to relate each of the 5 books of the Psalms to a particular book in the Pentateuch, or to see some over-riding theme in each section of the Psalms. None of those attempts has received general acceptance, and some of them have been quite fanciful. The fact is, each of the five books contains material greatly varied in theme and purpose. There does not seem to be any unifying factor common to each section, except that

  David is the author of most of the Psalms in the first two sections;

  Asaph is the reputed author of most of those in the third section;

  the Psalms of the fourth section are attributed to various authors;

  while those of the last are mainly anonymous.

- Perhaps the five books simply reflect earlier compilations upon which the whole collection was based (see (B) just below) -

  Books One and **Four** may have been compiled by David himself, some time prior to 970 B.C.:

  all but three (1, 9, 33) of the Psalms in *Book One* are attributed to David;

  Book Four ends with a Psalm (106) that draws from a Davidic Psalm (1 Ch 16:7,34-36); which may indicate David as its editor.

Book Four is more liturgical in nature, while ***Book One*** has a more personal character.

Since ***Book Three*** contains Psalms that refer to the fall of Jerusalem (74, 79, 89) it could not have been compiled before 586 B.C. (when Nebuchadnezzar finally captured the city), and may even have been gathered together during the exile in Babylon (cp. 74:9).

Book Five contains several post-exilic Psalms (note its opening lines in *Psalm 107:1-3*), so could not have been compiled before 537 BC (that is, after the Jews returned to Palestine after some 70 years of captivity in Babylon). Indeed, if *Psalm 147:2,6,12-14* may be read as a celebration of the rebuilding of the city, then Book Five may be dated as late as c. 440 BC.

♦ **ANCIENT SOURCES**

   – **CULTIC COLLECTIONS**

Some time after the return of the people from exile in Babylon, an editor (possibly Ezra or Nehemiah), brought together various ancient collections of Psalms into one corpus, for use in the temple of Zerubbabel (Ezr 5:1-2; Hg 1:14).

That collection must have been virtually identical to the one we now use, and it was generally well established by the time the LXX (the Greek version of the Old Testament) was published (c. 250 BC).

Thus there are a number of signs that our present collection of 150 Psalms is a compilation of several more ancient collections -

> We can show, for example, that Book Four must have been current when the Books of Chronicles were finally edited into their present form. The doxology that climaxes Book Four, was included by the chronicler when he quoted the last few verses of Psalm 106 in his composite Psalm in 1 Ch 16:8-36. That composite Psalm itself is made up from portions of Psalms 105, 96, and

106, all of which are from Book Four. So Book Four was apparently compiled prior to the time of Ezra.

Note the postscript to Book Two - "The prayers of David, the son of Jesse, are ended" (Ps 72:20). Does this mean that Psalm 72 was the last one ever composed by David, or was it simply the last song in a collection of Davidic poems? After all, a further 18 Psalms attributed to David follow this one, and a dozen Psalms by other authors come before it. This seems to indicate that Psalm 72 was at one time just the final poem in a separate collection of songs. Yet because he was the author of most of them, the entire collection was loosely attributed to David.

This particular collection may have comprised the first two Books of our present Psalter. Other Psalms, and the other books, were then added later to that collection, until it eventually reached its present size.

Even earlier, the first two books may have been used independently, as shown by the almost exact repetition of Psalms 14 & 40:13-17 (from Book One) in Psalms 53 & 70 (in Book Two).

In the same way, the latter parts of *Psalms 57 & 60* combine to create *Psalm 108* in **Book Five**; thus this Book too probably existed at one time as a separate collection.

Following the same practice, the hymn books used by various Christian denominations in our time contain many of the same hymns, along with those that are unique to each book.

The divine names Yahweh and Elohim occur nearly exclusively in different groups of Psalms. Thus:

> **Book One** prefers Yahweh, while **Book Two** prefers Elohim;
>
> most of **Book Three** (73-83) prefers Yahweh, but the remainder (84-89) prefers Elohim;

while in ***Books Four*** and ***Five*** Yahweh is used almost without exception.

Those changes seem to reflect the preferences of different cultic groups within Israel, each of which apparently had its own collection of sacred songs. Once again, much the same kind of thing can be seen today in the various Christian hymn books.[26]

– THE CHIEF MUSICIAN

Two groups of Psalms seem to have been special compilations, used by the directors of music in the Temple:

Psalms 42-49, are attributed to the Sons of Korah, which was an hereditary guild of temple officials and musicians

and *Psalms 73-83*, are attributed to Asaph, who was the founder of another of the Temple musical guilds.

Both of those collections may once have been separate from the main Psalter that was used by the people in the congregation.

– DIVIDED PSALMS

Psalms 9 & 10 make up one acrostic[27] poem, which for some reason was long ago broken into two separate songs.

Similarly, the repeated refrain in Psalms 42 & 43[28] shows that they were originally one Psalm, which was apparently early

---

[26] An illustration of this process can be seen in the changes that are introduced into some hymns to reflect the dogmas of a particular group. For example, the theological prejudice of one group causes it to change the wording of a gospel hymn from "When we all get to heaven ... " to "When we all see the kingdom ... " There are numerous similar examples.

[27] A poem in which each verse or line begins with successive letters of the alphabet. See below for further comment

[28] "Why are you cast down, O my soul, and why are you disquieted within me?" - Ps 42:5,11; 43:5.

divided into two songs. Why? Probably for some now unknown liturgical, practical, or theological purpose.

Note that neither Psalm 10 nor Psalm 43 have a separate title, suggesting once again that they were originally joined to their preceding Psalms. Such manipulations show the work of an unknown editor or compiler.

– **CLUSTERS OF PSALMS**

Books Four and Five have some other clusters, mostly linked by their subjects or uses rather than their authorship:

Psalms 93-100, which major on the world-wide kingship of the Lord

Psalms 113-118, the *"Egyptian Hallel"* ("praise"), which was sung each year on Passover night

Psalms 120-134, *"Songs of Ascents"* (perhaps meaning "pilgrimage"), which were part of the *"Great Hallel"* (120-136)

and a final *"Hallel"* consisting of *Psalms 146-150*, which all begin and end with *"Hallelujah!"*[29]

Note that the Psalter is climaxed by five *"Hallelujah"* Psalms, perhaps to create a five-fold doxology for the five-book collection.

There are also two later sets of Davidic Psalms (108-110 and 138-145), and the whole collection is prefaced by the anonymous Psalm 1, which may well have been composed for that express purpose.

THE MAJOR THEMES OF THE PSALTER

Someone has suggested that there are just three main themes in the Psalter

---

[29] Psalms 1-72, "Introduction;" in the Tyndale Old Testament Commentary. The Sections under (B) above are largely drawn from the same source.

- life revealing man's relationship with God
- nature revealing God's wisdom and power
- Israel revealing God's redemptive control of history
- Excellent as that suggestion may be, it seems a little artificial. At least we would have to say that subsidiary to those main themes the Psalms also focus upon
- the believer's confidence in God as Provider
- the inevitable doom of the ungodly
- predictions concerning the Messiah
- the sure triumph of the kingdom of God
- the inscrutable mysteries of divine providence
- the enthronement and reign of the king
- and many other occasional themes.

At least fourteen Psalms arise out of times of sickness, and express either thanksgiving for a cure, or complaint because healing had not come

see 6, 22, 30, 32, 38, 39, 41, 42-43, 51, 88, 102, 103, 116 - and perhaps others also.

Various other ways of grouping the Psalms can be found in the translations and commentaries. The following is a fairly standard list of the different types of Psalm -

> Hymns: songs of praise and worship, celebrating the glory of God and his mighty acts in heaven and on earth (e.g. Psalms 8, 103, 135, plus about 30 other Psalms).
>
> Laments: cries of supplication, prayers, entreaties, comprising at least 50 of the Psalms. You should note two important things about the Laments:
>
>> most of the *Laments* either contain a positive expression of faith, or end on one (although not all, for some of them end in despair - notably *Psalm 88*);

however they all reflect the pain and mystery that are part of the human condition, and they are just as important and just as necessary as the joyful songs.

Those factors make it necessary to read the entire Psalter, and not just the pleasant poems that tend to be found in "Promise Boxes" or collections of "Daily Devotions". Christians who focus only upon the happy promises of the Bible are setting themselves up for bewilderment when pain assails them, or when their hopes and dreams come crashing to the ground. The Psalms show that bitter disappointment, an apparently indifferent heaven, a silent God, is an inescapable part of the life of faith.

There are two kinds of lament:

> collective entreaties (e.g. Psalm 12); and
>
> individual entreaties (e.g. Psalm 13).

Thanksgiving: here we find both individual and collective songs of gratitude for some answered prayer or divine intervention, including at least Psalms 18, 21, 30, 33, 34, 40, 65-68, 92, 116, 118, 124, 129, 138, 144.

Prophetic: which either incorporate prophetic sayings or were composed out of expanded prophecies. The oracles found in these Psalms, whether short or long, may all have been originally spoken by a priest or prophet during the course of a Temple service (see Psalms 2, 50, 75, 81, 82, 85, 95, 110, etc.)

Wisdom: which reflect themes that are unusual for lyric poetry: upright living, the fear of God, dealing justly, etc. (see Psalms 1, 37, 49, 73, 91, 112, 127, 128, 133.)

Royal: connected with the monarchy of Israel, and dealing with various aspects of the king's life, enthronement, and reign (see Psalms 18, 20, 21, 28, 45, 61, 63, 72, 101, 132, 144.)

Messianic: which deal with the coming of the Messiah, his sufferings, and the glory to follow. Many (if not all) the Royal Psalms, along with some of the Prophetic Psalms, can obviously be applied to Christ; but other Psalms also have a messianic content: see Psalms 2, 8, 16, 22, 35, 40, 41, 45, 68, 69, 89, 72, 102, 110, 118, 119, 132.

Chapter Three

A STUDY IN POETRY

"There was some books ... full of beautiful stuff and poetry; but I didn't read the poetry."[30]

"I wish you would read a little poetry sometimes. Your ignorance cramps my conversation."[31]

There are two ways of using words, whether you are telling a story, expressing your feelings, describing a place, a thing, an event, or conveying an idea. The first is prose, which is the kind of speech we use every day, the writing style of newspapers, letters, novels, text books, ordinary conversation, and so on. Whether they realise it or not, everybody uses prose, as one of Moliere's[32] characters discovered to his great delight -

> M. Jourdain: What? When I say, "Nicole, bring me my slippers, and give me my night cap," is that prose?
>
> Philosophy Teacher: Yes, Sir.
>
> M. Jourdain: Good heavens! For more than forty years I have been speaking prose without knowing it![33]

So prose comes naturally to all of us. But there is another kind of writing, which we call poetry, and that is by no means natural. On the contrary, immense artistry, if not divine inspiration, is needed to write truly good poetry, that is, verses that are more than just a piece of literary wit, but speak to the deepest wellsprings of our being.

---

[30] Mark Twain, The Adventures of Huckleberry Finn (1884); Ch. 17.

[31] Anthony Hope (1863-1933), The Dolly Dialogues (1894) #22.

[32] 17th century French humorous playwright.

[33] Le Bourgeois Gentilhomme (1670); Act II, Sc. 4.

Alexander Pope[34] poured scorn on pretend poets who had more artifice than art, and he derided also their readers who had not the sense to realise that they were being fooled by verbal trickery -[35]

> But most by numbers judge a poet's song,
>
> And smooth or rough, with them, is right or wrong:
>
> In the bright Muse though thousand charms conspire,
>
> Her voice is all these tuneful fools admire;
>
> Who haunt Parnassus but to please their ear,
>
> Not mend their minds; as some to church repair,
>
> Not for the doctrine, but the music there.
>
> These equal syllables alone require,
>
> Though oft the ear the open vowels tire;[36]
>
> While expletives their feeble aid do join;
>
> And ten low words oft creep in one dull line: [37]
>
> . . . .
>
> Then, at the last and only couplet fraught
>
> With some unmeaning thing they call a thought,
>
> A needless Alexandrine[38] ends the song

---

[34] (1688-1744) English poet and literary critic

[35] There is here a useful caution for many would-be Christian poets who suppose that mere piety and zeal is a sufficient compensation for an utter lack of talent, toil, and tears. I have many times over the years had dreary verses thrust upon me by amateur bards who would not brook the least criticism or correction of their lamentable efforts. Seldom has any hopeful poet shown me lines that warrant even the effort of reading let alone preserving them.

[36] Two lines of biting satire, in which Pope himself emulates the "open vowels" he is criticising.

[37] A deliberately contrived dull line itself, containing ten words.

That, like a wounded snake, drags its slow length along.

. . . .

True ease in writing comes from art, not chance,

As those move easiest who have learned to dance.[39]

But does it matter? Why should you have any interest in poetry? For two reasons:

- *first*, for the sake of your own humanity, because poetry, like no other medium, can reach into the soul and stir the noblest ideas and emotions:

    "Poetry is the breath and finer spirit of all knowledge; it is the impassioned expression which is in the countenance of all science ... Poetry is the spontaneous overflow of powerful feelings: it takes its origin from emotion recollected in tranquillity."[40]

- *second*, for the sake of your spiritual growth, because so much of the Bible is poetry.[41]

The more familiar you are with poetry in general, the more deeply you will be able to enter into the poetry of the Bible and the more powerfully it will speak to you.

---

[38] A member of a group of wordy and tedious poets whom Pope scorned. The following line both echoes their ponderous style and conveys Pope's opinion of it.

[39] From An Essay on Criticism, which was an essay on styles of literature, but brilliantly written in verse, composed when Pope was only 20 years old.

[40] William Wordsworth (1770-1850), English poet, in a Letter to Lady Beaumont (May 21, 1807).

[41] Remember again the comments on this theme in Chapter One above.

THE EARLIEST LITERATURE

Have you ever realised that the earliest literature of all cultures is poetry? Hence the ancient Britons, long before they had any written language, welcomed to their homes and castles the wandering minstrels who sang in rhyme about the heroic deeds of brave men and women, whose example the hearers were urged to follow. Those ballads eventually became the first written literature, such us the 8th century Old English epic, Beowulf, which was the first major poem in a European vernacular tongue. Beowulf was a brave young hero who fought against monsters and dragons that were attacking his people. A strong thread of Christian comment and morality runs through its various episodes.

Likewise, the earliest literature of the old Greeks and Romans arose out of the minstrel songs that were sung around the firesides of their forefathers. Those ballads told the thrilling stories of the mighty warriors and adventurers whose exploits were thought to have laid the foundations of civilisation.

Similarly, the oldest parts of scripture are snatches of poetry, the ancient remains of Hebrew literature.[42]

"Poetry," as Johann Hamann[43] said, is indeed "the mother tongue of mankind." But that "mother tongue" is not the same in every culture, which brings us straight away to -

A TRANSLATION PROBLEM

- ♦ **RHYTHM AND RHYME**
    - Classical English poetry, apart from beauty of language and metaphor, depends for its effect mainly on the regular occurrence of rhyme and rhythm. Poets clothe their lines with the garment of rhythm, which they often garland also with rhyme. Those elements carry their words beyond an

---

[42] For a couple of examples, see Nu 21:14-15 & 17-18; Jsh 10:12-13.

[43] (1730-88) German philosopher and theologian, traveller and merchant, and writer.

appeal to the mind to compel a response from the heart - they stir the emotions; they grip the soul; they entice one into their embrace. Some English poetry ("blank" verse) may dispense with rhyme, but rhythm is usually thought necessary to distinguish poetry from prose. That distinction becomes obvious if you read aloud a prose paragraph (such as this one), followed by these lines from Alfred Noyes, "The Highwayman" -

> The wind was a torrent of darkness among the gusty trees,
> The moon was a ghostly galleon tossed upon cloudy seas,
> The road was a ribbon of moonlight over the purple moor,
> When the highwayman came riding - riding - riding -
> The highwayman came riding, up to the old inn door.

Who can escape the sense of being conveyed into that dusky scene, and of hearing the hoofbeats as the highwayman approaches the inn? Likewise, Robert Browning used a strong rhythm (along with rhyme) in his dramatic poem *How They Brought the Good News from Ghent to Aix* -

> I sprang to the stirrup, and Joris, and he;
> I galloped, Dirck galloped, we galloped all three;
> "Good speed!" cried the watch, as the gate-bolts undrew;
> "Speed!" echoed the wall to us galloping through;
> Behind shut the postern, the lights sank to rest,
> And into the midnight we galloped abreast

– But what about Hebrew poetry? Unlike most English poetry (at least in the past), Hebrew poetry only occasionally uses rhyme, but it often has a rhythm of sound, although the arrangement can be very flexible. Where such rhythms do occur, they are based on a succession of strong and weak syllables, with 3 stresses to a line being the most common; for example -

> Prove me, O Lord, and try me,
> Test Thou my heart and my mind.[44]

> Send out thy light and thy truth;
> Cause them to lead me, O God. [45]

- Nonetheless, the main feature of Hebrew poetry is not a repetition of sounds or of stress, but rather a repetition of ideas, which they arranged in many different ways. Sometimes they repeated the same idea in different words; sometimes they built one idea out of another; sometimes they contrasted different ideas; and so on (examples are given below).

This unique character of Hebrew poetry was first brought to the attention of the western world by the English bishop and scholar Robert Lowth, in a book he published in 1753. He called this poetic form parallelism. It was a startling discovery, and opened up wonderful possibilities in the interpretation of Israel's sacred songs and prophetic oracles.

♦ EMINENTLY TRANSLATABLE

2.2.1 The unique style of Hebrew poetry has made it eminently translatable into any language - unlike the poetry of most other nations (and certainly of English poetry), which always suffers badly in translation. Indeed, most foreign poetry, if it is to be any good (say) in English, must be heavily paraphrased. For example, Edward Fitzgerald's 19th century translation of the Ruba'iyat of Omar Khayyam[46] is an English masterpiece, but it bears little resemblance to the original, as the following comparisons will show-

---

[44] Ps 26:2.

[45] Ps 43:3.

[46] Omar Khayyam (c. 1050-1123) was a Persian astronomer, philosopher, mathematician, and poet, who served in the court of the sultan. In the western world his fame largely rested upon his work in mathematics, until in 1859 Fitzgerald produced his marvellous translation of Khayyam's sardonic quatrains. The "original" quatrains quoted above are from the translation by Peter Avery & John Heath-Stubbs; Penguin Books, London, 1983.

Fitzgerald -

> Here with a little Bread beneath the Bough,
> A Flask of Wine, a Book of Verse - and Thou
> Beside me singing in the Wilderness -
> Oh, Wilderness were Paradise enow!
>
> Quatrain 12

Original -

> I need a jug of wine and a book of poetry,
> Half a loaf for a bite to eat,
> Then you and I, seated in a deserted spot,
> Will have more wealth than a Sultan's realm.
>
> Quatrain 98[47]

Fitzgerald -

> Myself when young did eagerly frequent
> Doctor and saint, and heard great argument
> About it and about: but evermore
> Came out by the same door as in I went.
>
> With them the seed of Wisdom did I sow,
> And with my own hand wrought to make it grow:
> And this was all the Harvest that I reap'd -
> "I came like Water, and like Wind I go."
>
> Quatrains 30,31

---

[47] Of course, the original reads much more beautifully in its original Persian tongue.

Original

> When we were children we went to the Master for a time,
>
> For a time we were beguiled by our own mastery;
>
> Hear the end of the matter, what befell us:
>
> We came like water and we went like wind.
>
> Quatrain 37

Most readers think that Fitzgerald's translation is markedly better than Khayyam's original work, although the original quatrains probably read more liltingly in Persian than they do in a plain English rendering. But because of the restraints of rhythm and rhyme, in order to obtain anything like the effect of the Persian verses, a translator must take enormous liberties with the text.

- So it is a remarkable fact, and surely a mark of divine inspiration, that almost alone among the poetry of the world, the songs and the prayers of the Bible retain their full beauty and impact, no matter what language they are expressed in, and no matter how widely other literary forms and tastes may change from generation to generation. That is because ideas can be readily carried from one tongue to another, with little or no loss, whereas language structures may be almost impossible to convey across the barriers of culture and time.

- However, before looking at the Psalms in more detail, with their poetic parallelism, their rhythm of ideas, let us examine further the structure of English poetry. Showing the contrast between these two kinds of poetry will, I hope, intensify your appreciation of the extraordinary qualities possessed by the Psalms.

ENGLISH POETRY

3.1 CLASSICAL POETRY

- Standard English poetry is divided into various elements:

feet containing a fixed pattern of stressed syllables, with a set number of feet per line;

then **rhythm**, which depends upon the kind of "foot" that is used;

then **metre**, which is based upon the number of "feet" per line;

and English poetry is also usually divided into stanzas, each with a fixed number of lines;

and then the final element is rhyme - matching sounds at the end of lines, in various patterns.

The examples below show all those elements.[48]

- If you think about a few lines of printed music, you will see a similar kind of pattern - so many beats to the bar, so many bars to the measure, so many measures to the piece, and so on. You could think of the notes as syllables, the beat as a stressed syllable, the bars as feet, a measure as metre, a verse or chorus as a stanza or refrain, and so on.

  If you imagine a piece of music with no bars, no time, no rhythm, no formal structure, you would have the musical equivalent to prose.

- Coming back to poetry, a "foot" is a group of syllables, which each have a prescribed arrangement of strong and weak stresses. There are several such poetic "feet", which we have no need to learn about here, except that we could usefully look at a couple of examples -

    The "dactyl", which is a "foot" composed of three syllables, the first strong, the other two weak, thus,

---

[48] See also the Shakespeare Sonnet in Lesson One. In the collection of his sonnets, each poem has twelve lines, rhyming on alternate lines, and closing with two final lines, which rhyme with each other. Each line, including the last two, also has 10 syllables.

"DUM-dee-dee". That pattern can be seen and heard in the following lines -

<u>This</u> is the/ <u>for</u>est prim/ <u>ev</u>al. The/ <u>mur</u>muring/ <u>pines</u> and the/ <u>hem</u>locks."

<u>Take</u> her up/ <u>ten</u>derly/ <u>in</u>to your arms.

The "iambic", which is a "foot" composed of two syllables, the first weak, the second strong, thus "dee-DUM" -

The cur/few <u>tolls</u>/ the <u>knell</u>/ of <u>part</u>/ing day.

Fitzgerald's translation of the Ruba'iyat, *quoted above, is written in* iambic pentameter, *and each stanza is a* quatrain: *that is,*

each verse has four lines;

each line has five feet, in iambic rhythm (dee-DUM);

and the first, second, and fourth lines all rhyme.

Imagine how difficult it would be to translate each of those features accurately into another tongue! The task would probably be impossible, or else (like Fitzgerald's own work) the end result would be far more a paraphrase than a translation. Even worse; it would probably have to be a re-write, in which the translation bore only scant resemblance to the original poem. Ordinarily, rhythmic and rhyming poetry cannot be successfully carried from one tongue into another.

♦ MODERN POETRY

– In the 19th century a new kind of English poetry began to appear, which kept rhyme, but ignored foot and metre, and depended rather upon a fixed number of stressed syllables in each line. The main innovator of this style was the British poet, Gerard Manley Hopkins. Notice the four stressed syllables in each line in the following, from God's Grandeur -

The <u>world</u> is <u>charged</u> with the <u>grandeur</u> of <u>God</u>;
It will <u>flame</u> out, like <u>shin</u>ing from <u>shook foil</u>;

It <u>gath</u>ers to a <u>great</u>ness, like the <u>ooze</u> of <u>oil</u>
Crushed. Why do <u>men</u> then <u>now</u> not <u>reck</u> his <u>rod</u>?
Generations have <u>trod</u>, have <u>trod</u>, have <u>trod</u>;
And <u>all</u> is seared with <u>trade</u>; <u>bleared</u>; smeared with <u>toil</u>;
And wears <u>man's</u> <u>smudge</u>, and shares <u>man's</u> <u>smell</u>: the soil
Is <u>bare</u> now, nor can <u>foot</u> <u>feel</u>, being <u>shod</u>.

Note how in line 7 (for example), knowing the pattern of the poem helps you to decide how to read it; that is, you will be led to emphasise *"man's"* smudge and smell, which obliterate the natural colour and fragrance of the earth.

– The same four stresses per line can be found in W. H. Auden's Epitaph On A Tyrant

<u>Perfec</u>tion, of a <u>kind</u>, was <u>what</u> he was <u>after</u>,
And the <u>poet</u>ry he in<u>vent</u>ed was <u>easy</u> to under<u>stand</u>;
He <u>knew</u> human <u>folly</u> like the <u>back</u> of his <u>hand</u>,
And was <u>greatly</u> <u>interested</u> in <u>armies</u> and <u>fleets</u>;
When <u>he</u> laughed, res<u>pect</u>ed senators <u>burst</u> with <u>laughter</u>,
And when he <u>cried</u> the little <u>child</u>ren <u>died</u> in the <u>streets</u>.

Again, reading the poem with the correct stress highlights the dramatic horror of the last two lines.

– From that kind of freer poetry developed an even looser form, based not on stress but only on the number of syllables in each line, as in this verse from Thom Gunn's (American, 1929 -) poem, "The Snail" -

The snail pushes through a green
night, for the grass is heavy
with water and meets over

the bright path he makes, where rain
has darkened the earth's dark. He

moves in a wood of desire,
pale antlers barely stirring
as he hunts.

- From that again there evolved the kind of blank verse that has no fixed number of feet, stresses, syllables, or even rhyme, and could in fact be written as prose. It gains its poetic shape either from a certain sense of rhythm or of balance in the lines, or simply from the way the poet chooses to arrange the lines on the page, as in much of the poetry currently printed in literary journals.

Against that background, it is now time to look more closely at the remarkable structure of Hebrew poetry.

Chapter Four

A BEAUTY OF IDEAS

INTRODUCTION

— When the nature of English poetry is understood, the ways in which it differs from Hebrew poetry not only become immediately apparent, but also important for highlighting the unique character of the Psalms. I have already shown the nearly impenetrable difficulty of translating into another language poetry that depends for its effect upon a symmetry of sound. In general, such poetry can be translated effectively only by putting it into prose, or else drastically re-writing it (as Fitzgerald did to the Ruba'iyat).

Another example can be found in the various translations of Homer's[49] *Iliad* and *Odyssey*. For example, here are the opening lines of the *Iliad*, first in fairly literal verse form, then in Alexander Pope's[50] translation, then in a prose version by E. V. Rieu (a modern author) -

"Sing, goddess, the wrath of Peleus' son Achilles,

---

[49] "Homer" is the name given to the actually unknown author(s) of the two great epic Greek poems, the "Iliad" and the "Odyssey", that were composed possibly as early as the 10th century before Christ. The "Iliad" tells the renowned story of the Greek conquest of Troy, c. 1200 BC The "Odyssey" tells the story of the long voyage taken by the hero Odysseus, his many adventures, and his eventual return to claim his faithful wife Penelope.

[50] Alexander Pope (1688-1744), English poet, satirist, political commentator, and moralist, translated Homer across many years of arduous labour, and produced a masterpiece that many critics think surpassed the original in its poetic splendour.

> A destroying wrath that brought upon the Achaeans myriad woes."

> "Achilles' wrath, to Greece the direful spring
>
> Of woes unnumbered, heavenly goddess, sing!"

> "The Wrath of Achilles is my theme, that fatal wrath which ... brought the Achaeans so much suffering ... Let us begin, goddess of song, with the angry parting that took place .... "

Notice how the prose version is longer than either verse translation, but more accurately conveys the sense of the original Greek. An English verse translation, which attempts to copy the cadence and rhythm of Homer, can be made only at the cost of losing many of the nuances of the original. Conversely, only abandoning any attempt to present the translation in verse form can retain those nuances.

By contrast with such problems, Hebrew poetry is generally much more flexible, for it is based, not on a symmetry of *sounds*, but rather on a symmetry of *ideas*. It is thus readily translatable, without loss of beauty or sense, into any other language.

> – Another point of difference between Hebrew poetry and ordinary English poetry is its lack of regular stanzas. Usually the poetical passages in the Bible are single units, without any observable strophic form;[51] however, there are exceptions, namely
>
>> the several acrostic Psalms[52]

---

[51] That is, lacking any pattern of regular or identical stanzas.

[52] That is, poems in which each new line or verse begins with the successive letters of the alphabet. Section (II)(C)(1)(c) below discusses the nine commonly recognised Acrostic Psalms. There are at least another five alphabetic passages in the Old Testament, but none in the New Testament.

the Psalms in which a refrain occurs (42, 43, 46, 49, 107, 136, etc.)

the Psalms in which *selah* occurs, for, among other things, *selah* may have been used to mark off a strophe.[53]

Nonetheless, even in such strophic Psalms, the stanzas are usually uneven and irregular, for again the Hebrew poet was always more interested in ideas than he (or she) was in mere structure.

— Before we look at the three major characteristics of Hebrew poetry, you should notice another significant idea -

AN IMPORTANT FACTOR

♦ VITAL FOR UNDERSTANDING

Discovering the structure of Hebrew poetry is not just a curious exercise, rather, it is essential for a proper understanding of the Psalms. In this respect most modern translations are helpful, because they print the poetical passages of scripture in such a way as to separate them clearly from those parts that are prose.

Does that really matter?

Yes, because if you read a piece of poetry in the same way as you would a piece of prose, you will almost certainly falsify the meaning of the poetry.

Think again about English poetry for a moment, and how you adopt a different mental attitude when you approach poetry. You would not think of reading it the same way as you do the morning newspaper. Words, ideas, have different meanings, are used in different ways, in poetry. Consider, for example, these lines from John Donne's *The Anniversary* -

> Here upon earth, we are kings, and none but we
>
> Can be such kings, nor of such subjects be;

---

[53] A strophe is a section of a poem, usually consisting of several stanzas, and often irregular in length.

> Who is so safe as we? where none can do
> Treason to us, except one of us two.
> True and false fears let us refrain,
> Let us love nobly, and live, and add again
> Years unto years, till we attain
> To write threescore, this is the second of our reign.

Donne there uses the figure of speech I mentioned above,[54] a poetic *conceit* - that is, an illustrative device in which he likens a recently wedded couple to royal monarchs. He calls their marriage a kingdom, and their years together a reign. The *conceit* employed in *The Anniversary* is fairly simple; in some of his other poems Donne uses much more subtle and elusive devices, which for that reason are all the more fascinating. But the point to notice is that the poem cannot be understood until the *conceit* is penetrated and its words are given meanings other than usual. For example -

> And now good morrow to our waking souls,
>   Which watch not one another out of fear;
> For love, all love of other sights controls,
>   And makes one little room an everywhere.
> Let sea-discoverers to new worlds have gone,
>   Let maps to others, worlds on worlds have shown,
>   Let us possess one world, each hath one, and is one.
>
> My face in thine eye, thine in mine appears,
>   And true plain hearts do in the faces rest,
> Where can we find two better hemispheres
>   Without sharp north, without declining west?

---

[54] In Chapter One.

> Whatever dies, was not mixed equally;
>
> If our two loves be one, or, thou and I
>
> Love so alike, that none do slacken, none can die.[55]

At a time when Europeans were still busy exploring the oceans of the world, discovering new seas and continents, the poet uses the *conceit* of likening himself and his beloved to the two hemispheres of the globe, which, joined together, become a single earth. Yet in their case it is a world without the frigid north of fading desire, nor the setting sun of love's decay; it is a world free of betrayal or mistrust, because their love gives them eyes only for each other. Nor do they envy those adventurous explorers and map-makers; for to these lovers even one small room seems larger than the universe. They find more joy in the discovery of each other than navigators do in finding a new world.

The same principle of interpretation is true of Hebrew poetry. The Psalms abound in similes, metaphors, hyperbole, imagery - indeed the whole range of what is often called "poetic license". They cannot reasonably be read and interpreted as though they were sober prose. Beneath the rich and flowing language the true intent of the poet must be discerned.

♦ PAST THE HEAD TO THE HEART

The above factors have led commentators to make remarks like those of Dr W. J. Martin -

> "The rhythm of Hebrew poetry is not the measured beat of the earth-bound body. It is the majestic rhythm of the soaring spirit, felt only by those who have the music of heaven within their souls. It rises above the rhetorical to a loftier plane and to a new dimension - the dimension of the spirit, where they who worship God worship him in spirit and in truth."[56]

Hence it can be said that the Psalms complement the other parts of scripture by providing for our emotional and inner spiritual life and guidance what

---

[55] The Good Morrow, second and third stanzas.

[56] I have lost the source of this quote.

those other parts provide for our faith and actions. In the Psalter prayer is revealed in all of its possible forms and content; here we find the deepest dramas of the faith life, an intimate insight into the finest joys and the darkest sorrows of striving to live godly in a fallen world.

Nevertheless, while the Psalms are often *impassioned* they are not *unstructured*; for all their depth of feeling, the psalmists were still careful when they entered the presence of God (Ec 5:1-2), and they expressed that reverence through careful composition -

THE STRUCTURE OF THE PSALMS

There are gaps in our knowledge of the forms of ancient Hebrew poetry, and scholars still debate various points. Nonetheless, there is no longer any doubt about the general structure of the Psalms, which can be said to have three main common characteristics -

♦ PARALLELISM

The term *parallelism* is used to describe the dominant feature of Hebrew poetry, which we have seen is the matching of *ideas* rather than *sounds*. This feature has also been called "thought rhyme", in contrast with the "word rhyme" that characterises most other poetry.

Scholars differ considerably in the terms they use to describe the various kinds of parallelism found in the Bible. The following suggestions are an amalgamation of the forms adopted by the several commentators I have been able to check -

– TYPES OF PARALLELISM

The Hebrews created many varieties of parallelisms:

synonymous: where the first statement is repeated more or less exactly by the second - 114; 22:27-29; 46:1,7; 59:1,2; 82:1-4; 92:12-14; etc.

synthetic: where the second statement complements the first, carrying its thought further and completing it - 14:2a; 21:1-2; 27:6a; 55:6; 92:1-4; etc.

antithetic: where the second statement expresses a contrast to the first (this is the dominant form of many of the sayings in Proverbs and in the teaching of Jesus, cp. Mt 7:18; 10:39) - 1:6; 30:5; 32:10; 37:21; etc.

climactic: where the second statement amplifies the effect of the first, echoing or repeating part of it, and carrying it forward to completion - 29:1,5,6,8,10-11; 55:12,13; 121:1-4; etc.

consecutive: where the first statement serves as the base upon which the second rests (a cause and effect relationship) - 19:7-10; 22:4-5,6-8; 99:1-4; etc.

emblematic: where the first statement is literal, and the second repeats it in figurative form - 103:11-13; etc.

introverted: where the form is more complex than the simple couplet construction exhibited in most of the examples cited above. There is an almost endless variety of possible arrangements, like the following:

> Psalm 30:8-10, where couplets 1&4 and then 2&3 are parallel;
>
> Psalm 135:15-18, where couplets 1&4 are parallel, then lines 3&6, and 4&5;
>
> Psalm 51:1, where lines 1&4 are parallel, then lines 2&3;
>
> Psalm 24:7-10, where lines 1-3 parallel lines 7-9; then lines 4-6 parallel lines 10-12.

A particular form of introverted parallelism is called chiasm,[57] because it is thought to resemble the Greek letter χ (*chi*) or the shape of a cross –

---

[57] Pronounced "kai-asm".

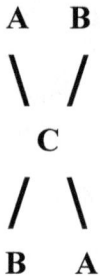

Here is an example of a different chiastic pattern from *Psalm 37* -

- A. Do not fret because of the wicked, nor envy those who do wrong
- B. They will soon wither like grass, and wilt like a plucked flower
- C. Trust in the Lord and do good, and you will enjoy long life and peace
- D. Delight yourself in the Lord and he will give you your heart's desire
- D. Commit your way to the Lord, and he will respond to your trust
- C. He will vindicate your righteousness like the brightness of the dawn
- B. Be still before the Lord and wait patiently for him
- A. Do not fret over those who prosper when they carry out their evil plans.

There are scores of other places in the Psalms where such *chiastic*[58] patterns can be seen. They are in fact scattered throughout the Bible, for chiasm was a common device of the Hebrews. For Christians, it is fascinating to see this shadow of the cross permeating the whole Bible.

---

[58] Pronounced "kai-as'-tic".

A striking Old Testament example of a chiastic parallel can be found in *Numbers 23:7-10*, which follows the pattern A-B-C-C-B-A.

A New Testament example is embedded in *Romans 2:17-20*, which follows the pattern A-B-C-D-E-AA-BB-CC-DD-EE; however, one needs a discerning eye to discern such complex patterns!

Few of the Psalms, of course, are confined to one style of parallelism; in most of them several forms are combined.

> see for example *Psalm 78*, in which two introductory sections (vs. 1-4 and 5-8) are each built around a long series of parallel statements;
>
> then comes a series of *couplets* (9-30), climaxed by a *triplet* (31);
>
> that is followed by a series of *couplets* in vs. 32-37, with a climax in 38 & 39; then *couplets* (40-44) climaxed in 49-51; then *couplets* in 52-72.

– UNITS OF VERSE

The normal unit of Hebrew verse is the "couplet" (Psalm 19:1) - or, more technically, a *distich*, from a Greek expression meaning "two lines." However, there are many variations:

> *monostich* (single line): 18:1; 87:1.
>
> *tristich* (three lines): 1:1; 5:11; 45:1; 100:1.
>
> *tetrastich* (four lines): 1:3; 55:21.
>
> *pentastich* (five lines): 6:6-7.
>
> *hexastich* (six lines): 99:1-3.
>
> and sometimes even more lines, as in 80:8-11

♦ METER

The *thought-rhyme* of the Psalms is complemented in the Hebrew text by various rhythmical patterns, based on the number of stressed syllables to the line. The most common of these rhythms is created by couplets employing three accents per line (3+3); for example

> <u>Yah</u>weh my <u>Sheph</u>erd <u>is</u>,
>
> Nothing shall I lack;
>
> In <u>pas</u>tures of <u>green</u> <u>grass</u>
>
> He makes me lie down.

or another example, from Psalm 121

> I <u>raise</u> my <u>eyes</u> to the <u>hills</u>,
>
> From <u>whence</u> shall <u>come</u> my <u>help</u>?
>
> My <u>help</u> shall <u>come</u> from <u>Yah</u>weh
>
> The <u>maker</u> of <u>heaven</u> and <u>earth</u>.

but many variations occur, such as the 3+3+3 pattern in *Psalm 24:7* -

> Lift-up || O-gates || your-heads!
>
> Be-rais'd || O-doors || eternal!
>
> Let-come || the-king || of-glory.
>
> Who-is || this-king || of-glory?
>
> Yah-weh || strong-and || might-y
>
> Yah-weh || strong-in || battle![59]

Knowledge of the metrical patterns in the Psalms is often a help to translators who are trying to repair a defective text; scholars can guess what word or syllables may be missing, based on the pattern of the surrounding lines. Knowledge of the meter of a Psalm may also occasionally assist in the interpretation of a difficult passage. However, such knowledge is obviously available only to those who are deeply familiar with biblical Hebrew. For those who must read the Bible in translation it remains inaccessible. Its main interest for us is to demonstrate that the psalms were not spontaneous

---

[59] The arrangement of the Hebrew syllables in the above passages differs from the English rendering given, which is simply an attempt to convey the feel of the original.

effusions, the products of immediate and urgent inspiration, but carefully crafted poems, comprising some of the greatest poetry ever written.

- ♦ **ARRANGEMENT**
  - **THREE MAJOR PATTERNS**

    Many of the Psalms are arranged around a distinct pattern -

    ### Refrains

    These are Psalms where a certain line or stanza is repeated on a regular basis:

    > see 42:5,11 & 43:5; the refrain indicates that these two Psalms were once a single poem, but were later divided - possibly for liturgical purposes;

    > see 46:7,11; it seems probable that the same refrain once followed verse3, but was dropped by accident somewhere in the distant past;

    > see also 49:12,20; 57:5,11; 99:3,5,9 ("Holy is He"); 107:6,8,13, etc; 136:1b,2b,3b, etc.

    ### Antiphony

    These are Psalms composed for responsive chanting or singing; that is, choir and congregation might alternate in singing certain lines; or a temple cantor might provide the lead, with the congregation or the choir responding at set points in the song; and so on.

    > ***see Psalm 115***, which is a capsule of a larger liturgy, which some commentators would divide as follows:
    >
    > > (1-2) an opening statement by a choir
    > > (3-8) a soloist scorns the worship of idols
    > > (9-11) the choir exhorts the people to trust God
    > > (12-13) a response by the congregation
    > > (14-15) a priest pronounces the blessing
    > > (16-18) concluding hymn of praise.
    >
    > ***see Psalm 118***, which some commentators would divide as follows:

(1) the call to worship, by the cantor, or choir
(2-4) the cantor bids each group to sing the refrain
(5-7) the psalmist, perhaps the king, recounts his experience of battle and God-given victory
(8-9) an official, perhaps a priest or a prophet, delivers an admonition to the praying monarch
(10-14) the king resumes his prayer with more confidence
(15-16) a prophet delivers an exultant oracle
(17-18) the king responds with a humble affirmation

(Up to this moment the ceremony appears to have taken place outside the temple, because now, the procession having reached the great gates ...)

(19) the king asks to be admitted to the temple
(20) a cantor, priest, or ceremonial guard standing within calls back that only those who are righteously qualified may enter
(21-22) the sovereign answers that God had borne witness to his character by delivering him even though others had rejected him
(23-24) the choir or congregation joyously tell what God has done
(25) a prayer is interjected
(26-27a) the suppliant is admitted with a choral blessing
(27b) perhaps a liturgical instruction that slipped into the text
(28) the king offers a prayer of thanksgiving
(29) concluding hymn of praise.

*see **Psalm 136**,* in which the cantor probably sang the first part of each verse, and the people the refrain.

Acrostics

The Hebrews frequently made use of acrostic poems, in which the initial letters of each line, couplet, or stanza were made to follow in sequence the 22 letters of the Hebrew alphabet. It is very difficult to maintain the sequence without becoming stilted or artificial, so translators seldom attempt to carry the acrostic pattern into English. However, in our language an acrostic Psalm might look like this:

> **A**ll that is within me offers praise to God and reverence to his holy name.
>
> **B**less the Lord without ceasing all you who love the Lord, the Saviour of Israel.
>
> **C**all upon him with tireless joy and trust, for his promise is worthy of faith.
>
> **D**elight yourself in the Lord; for who can measure the bounty he offers his servants?
>
> **E**ternal joys are his promise, and his right hand strengthens all who love him truly.
>
> **F**ar away he has cast our sins, but close at hand he has placed the countless gifts of his grace.

Why did the psalmists attempt such an exacting task? Perhaps as a mnemonic device, or out of a sense of artistry, or, more likely, to convey the sense of *completeness*. In the latter case, the idea would be akin to our saying, *"Everything from A-Z!"* So acrostic Psalms may be an attempt to make a complete statement about such human experiences as grief, joy, hope, trust, righteousness, devotion, and the like.

Among the Psalms, nine are generally recognised as being acrostic *or "alphabetic" in form:*[60]

> **Psalm 111, 112**, where each line begins with a different letter of the alphabet;

---

[60] You might find it an interesting exercise to try to alphabetize in English a few verses from these acrostic psalms, using the same pattern as the ancient poet did.

Psalms 25, 34, 145, where each couplet begins with a different letter;

Psalm 119, which is divided into 22 sections, each containing 8 couplets; each section represents a letter in the Hebrew alphabet and each of the couplets within a section begin with the letter belonging to that section;

Psalms 9, 10, where the acrostic pattern is continued from one Psalm to the other, thus indicating that they were once a single poem;[61]

Psalm 37, where again (like Psalms 9 & 10) the acrostic pattern is incomplete, which suggests that the original Psalm has been damaged in transmission; the pattern is that of beginning each stanza with a new letter.

Other factors

Hebrew poetry uses the rhetorical devices common to poetry everywhere; such as

exaggerated figures of speech (Ps 80:8-13)

hyperbole (91:7)

repetition of ideas or words from line to line (29:1-2,3-9)

similes (102:3-6)

alliteration of words and sounds (in the Hebrew text)

and various other manners of speech.

A careful reader will be alert for such poetic freedoms, and will avoid making them mean more than they intend.

---

[61] The pattern in the two latter Psalms is that of beginning each stanza with a new letter. However, the pattern is incomplete, which suggests that the original poem has been damaged in transmission.

Chapter Five

ANGRY PSALMS

A number of the Psalms contain cruel curses that offend sensitive readers -

> "Lord, throw your spear and javelin at those who chase me ... Let terrible disasters fall upon them; catch them in the net they set for me; plunge them into an abyss of ruin!"

> "O God, smash their faces in! May they melt away into their own slime, like creeping slugs. Make them like an aborted fetus, unfit to live, never to see the light of day!"

> "Roast my enemies on the spit of your anger, O Lord; burn them into a heap of ashes!"

> "Tear out the eyes of my foes, and leave them to grope in darkness, while their guts cramp with terror. Swamp them under the floodtide of your anger; utterly crush them with Your fury. Show them no pity as you add punishment to punishment, and never turn a tender eye toward them. Blot them totally out of the roll of those who deserve to live; never let them be numbered among the righteous!"

> "When my enemy is dragged into court, O God, turn every witness into a perjurer against him. Make sure he is found guilty. If he prays to you, treat even his petition as a sin. Cut his life short! Let all his possessions be stolen! Turn his children into orphans, and make his wife a widow. I want to see his children ragged and hungry, driven out of even the worst hovels. Oh that the moneylenders would seize everything he owns! Oh that robbers might snatch the bread right out of his mouth! Make sure that no one ever shows him any kindness, no, not even to pity his fatherless children!"

See 35:3-8; 58:6-10; 59:12-13; 69:22-28; 109:6-15; 137:7-9; and similar imprecatory passages can also be found in Psalms 5, 7, 18, 28, 54, 55, 79, 83, 101, 139.

The bitter denunciations, the fierce vindictiveness, found in such passages seem to be contrary to the message of the gospel. How could such harsh words have been inspired by the Holy Spirit? Indeed, some people have denied the authority of the Bible just because they take offence at the imprecatory Psalms. Shall we follow them? Hardly! Yet those angry Psalms do pose an ethical dilemma. How shall we solve it?

Some or all of the following suggestions may be taken as a sufficient solution to the problem -

AN OLDER ETHIC

♦ DON'T JUDGE TOO HASTILY

Honest readers will not make the mistake of pulling ethical standards out of only one part of scripture; the witness of the whole Bible must be taken into account. With that in mind, remember that the supposed difficulty caused by the imprecatory Psalms arises from the Bible itself. That is, later passages of scripture are the source of that same higher ethic that causes us to shrink from the imprecatory Psalms! Now the authors of those later passages knew about the imprecatory Psalms, but were apparently undisturbed by them - see, for example, *Acts 1:20*, which quotes *Psalm 69:25* and *109:8*; and *Romans 11:9-10*, which quotes *Psalm 69:22-23*. Paul had obviously found a way to accommodate the violence of those Psalms to the gracious message of Christ.

We can make a similar accommodation simply by remembering that manners and verbal expressions tend to be milder and more restrained today than they were in those more primitive times. Perhaps the rough terms used by the psalmists were intended to convey no more than is conveyed by our gentler forms of speech. We accept, for example, that the psalmists used soaring extravagance when they expressed their praise and worship of God, and we instinctively reduce those exaggerated declarations to more realistic proportions. The same reductions may fairly be applied to passages that express extremes of rage and grief.

The ancient Hebrews differed markedly from us in their love of

♦ A HYPERBOLIC STYLE

In our culture, we are prone to agree with Francis Bacon (c. 1600) that *"Speaking in a perpetual hyperbole is comely in nothing but in love!"* Consequently, we tolerate the excessive language of *The Song of Solomon* (which is a collection of love songs), but we become unsure of ourselves when we encounter the same fulsome speech in passages that we feel should be read more literally. Do those passages actually mean what they say, or must we modify their language? The Hebrews had no such problem; they were accustomed to hyperbole in every part of their speech, and made the necessary adjustments without any conscious effort. Hence, in *Acts 17:6*, the Jewish zealots rather wildly denounced the apostles as men *"who had turned the world upside down"*; and Paul himself was hardly sluggish when he claimed that the gospel had been *"preached to every creature under heaven"*! (Cl 1:6,23).

Following on from the preceding paragraphs, the use of hyperbole in the ancient world seems to have been particularly associated with ritual curses, without any serious intention that the curse should be literally fulfilled. For example, how literally are we to take the shocking words,

> "Oh what happiness to take your little ones and dash them to pieces against a rock!"? (Ps 137:9)

Did Jeremiah really mean it when he said,

> "Condemn their children to die of starvation; let them be murdered by the sword!"? (Je 18:21)

Did Isaiah truly believe Babylon would become so desolate that

> "wild beasts will lie down there, and its houses will be full of howling creatures; there ostriches will dwell, and there satyrs will dance"? (Is 13:21)

Were such awful curses meant to be fulfilled in every detail, or were they simply contemporary idioms, intended to convey only a general sense of retribution for wrongdoing? An examination of the writings of Israel's neighbours shows that such curse-formulae were common in the ancient world, and they were used with no idea that they would actually happen. They were just as hyperbolic as modern sayings like, *"Shoot me if I'm wrong,"* or, *"May a thousand plagues strike him!"*

The major difference between the ancients and us is *that we use such extreme sayings only in an informal or jocular setting*; but the *Hebrews used them in formal settings*, such as worship, commerce, and politics. Here are two examples from the secular world of ancient Mesopotamia. The first comes from a curse attached to an oath of allegiance demanded from court officials -

> "May Sarpanitu, who gives name and seed, destroy your name and seed ... May Adad, controller of the waters of heaven and earth dry up your ponds ... with a great flood may he submerge your land ... May want and famine, hunger and plagues never be removed from you."

And then, second, from a curse attached to a treaty of alliance between two cities -

> "May the gods send every sort of devourer against Arpad and against its people ... May its vegetation be destroyed unto desolation, and may Arpad become a mound to house the desert animal and the gazelle and the fox and the hare and the wild cat and the owl ... May this city never be mentioned again!"[62]

Did the makers of those treaties really suppose that such dreadful blights would fall upon any violator? Surely not; the intention was rather to enhance the solemnity of the covenant, and to promise some kind of severe retribution upon anyone who broke it. What form that retribution would actually take would depend upon time and circumstance, and the intervention of the gods.

Of course, we today would not use such violent language to seal a commercial treaty, nor a political alliance, nor in association with a religious vow or a prophecy, but the peoples of the ancient world did do so. Our task then, since our language contains no similar idioms, is **first** *to translate the curses literally, and* **second** *to try to determine what they meant to those who spoke them.*

---

[62] The above examples of "curse-formulae", and those that are given below, were taken from an article by G. G. Garner, in the March 1973 issue of <u>Buried History</u> magazine.

Thus, in the case of the fearful dooms pronounced against Babylon, it seems that the intention of the prophets was adequately fulfilled when the city was captured by Cyrus in 539 B.C. Nebuchadnezzar's glittering empire collapsed, never to rise again.[63] The subsequent fluctuating fortunes of the city itself, its eventual disappearance, and its present rebuilding by Iraq, are all irrelevant to the judgments pronounced in scripture.

The same kind of interpretation should probably be given to other pagan curses as the following -

> "May your wives be stripped naked, and the wives of your offspring be left with no garments" (cp. Je 3:26).
>
> "May your bow be broken" (cp. Je 49:35).
>
> "May there be no milk or oven in your house ... may they grind your bones and those of your sons and daughters" (cp. Je 25:10; 13:14; Ez 23:25).
>
> "May a pregnant mother and her daughter eat the flesh of your sons ... in hunger may one man eat the flesh of another" (cp. Je 19:9; Ez 5:10).

When you see the prophets echoing so closely the curse formulae used by their pagan neighbours, the conclusion becomes almost inescapable that this was a common manner of speaking in the ancient world. This means that such idioms should not be taken any more literally than we do the popular sayings and slang expressions used in our own culture.

If that is so, then God's justice was not obliged to perform every detail of the curses. On the contrary, the people presumably expected that the penalty imposed by heaven would in fact be suited to the degree of vileness of the crime and to the circumstances in which the violation occurred. In other words, whatever the curse threatened, the Lord would be fair and impartial in his judgments.

---

[63] Babylon was still a flourishing commercial centre 800 years later, in the time of Jesus. Soon after, because of changing trade routes, it began to decline, and was finally abandoned around the year 200 AD, a thousand years after Isaiah had cursed it!

GOD'S WAYS ARE RIGHTEOUS

♦ AN ANCIENT BOOK

When considering the *curse-formulae*, remember that the Bible is an ancient book, born in a culture very different from ours; it is therefore foolish to read scripture the same way you would a book written only yesterday. Before we can truly know what scripture means for us we must first get as close as we can to what it meant for its contemporaries. Here are some suggestions to that end -

- Psalm 139:21-22. The underlying idea here, and in many similar passages, is not so much one of personal vengeance as of zeal for the Lord. Behind the written curse stands a belief that God, to be just, must distinguish between right and wrong, and that judgment as well as mercy must characterise God's dealings with men (see also 58:11).

- Psalm 109 is a noteworthy example of this principle. The "enemy" being cursed by David is probably Saul, yet in real life David often forgave Saul and refused to do him any harm (cp. vs. 3-5). Plainly then, David's terrible imprecations were not motivated by any personal desire for revenge, but rather for God to vindicate his own righteousness and to uphold the integrity of his covenant with David.

Yet still the question might be raised: "Why such furious vehemence?" Here is another suggestion: the savage and disturbing language of such passages as *Psalm 109:6-19* may result from a desire by the psalmist to provide a counter-curse strong enough to repel the black-magic curses of his enemy (note vs. 2,17-18; and cp. 58:3-6). Perhaps it had come to the psalmist's ears that his enemy had pronounced a solemn curse against him, so he felt it necessary to erect a verbal barrier against that venomous attack.

Yet there remained a profound difference between the psalmist and his enemy, who undoubtedly believed that his curse itself had a magical power to harm the servant of God. Not so the psalmist. He knew that his malediction would have no effect apart from the intervention of God; he had no superstitious belief in the power of mere words to harm another. So he added to his curse a prayer of humble petition (109:20-31), trusting that God would *"deal well"* with him and *"deliver"* him from his foe.

♦ PROPHETIC ORACLES

Many of the imprecatory passages are *prophetic*; that is, they were not written to express the actual wish of the psalmist, but to declare things that were going to happen -

- Thus Psalm 137:8-9 may simply be describing the historical joy of the pagan (not Israelite) armies that overthrew great Babylon. The psalmist may not have been expressing any personal pleasure in the brutal murder of infants, but vividly portrayed the exultant cruelty of soldiers aroused to an awful blood-lust by the wild stimulus of war.
- In addition, the grammatical voice, mood, and tense of Hebrew verbs can be ambiguous, and it often becomes a matter of choice whether the translator reads a verb as "May God destroy him;" or, "God will destroy him":

    thus some read Psalm 125:5 as, "But those who turn to crooked ways the Lord <u>will banish with the evildoers" (NIV); while others read it as, "But those who turn aside into crooked ways,</u> may the Lord destroy them, as he destroys all evildoers!" (NEB).

- If most such passages should be read as prophecies, rather than as prayers, then much of the moral dilemma is removed from them.

♦ A FUTURE HOPE

At the time the Psalms were written there was still no really developed doctrine of a future resurrection and judgment in which all men would be requited for their deeds. The people of those days had at best only a shadowy hope of *personal resurrection*; their main faith was centred on God's continuing purpose for the *nation*. The focus of their hope was God's promise of future glory for the state of Israel. Therefore, if righteousness was to be vindicated and the ungodly punished, it had to take place in this life.

Because of our assured hope of the resurrection and of the awesome judgment that will follow, we speak vigorously about the *future* bliss of the godly and the *future* torment of the ungodly. But the psalmists, believing generally that God's justice had to be revealed now or never, insisted that it should be enacted without delay.

♦ JUSTICE IS STERN

The Psalms were written during a hard age (cp. 2 Sa 12:31), when cruelty and violence were an unhappy part of life. It was inevitable that the biblical authors should reflect the character of the societies in which they lived. However, while the Bible does record the brutality of the times, that does not constitute an endorsement of such violence. Indeed, the New Testament reflects a much gentler ethic, which has now become the standard for Christians to follow.

The imprecatory Psalms may be read then, not as declaring some *personal vindictiveness*, but rather as displaying a *judicial concern* to see evil eradicated from the land and the ways of righteousness fully established. Such bans then become the sentences of a judge who has sworn to uphold the law, or of a king sworn to protect his subjects. Leaders with militant responsibilities may, and should, pray for success in their tasks, just as those do who are engaged in more peaceful occupations.

Remember also that the maledictory passages are all prayers, and insofar as a person is responsible for the destruction of evil and for the upholding of just law, then it is right for such a person to echo the righteously wrathful sentiments of the kings and warriors of Israel.

A final thought: some people try to remove the problem of the imprecatory Psalms by seeing in them a prophecy of an event they expect in the future: *The Great Tribulation*. In this view, the "enemy" becomes a picture of *The Man of Sin*, that is, of the *Antichrist*, and of his henchmen. It is then said that no imprecations are too terrible to heap upon the head of this coming *Beast*! But placing the problem into the future in no way solves it. If it is immoral now to pray such prayers, then it will be equally immoral in the future, no matter what the circumstances may be. It is better to find a solution to the problem of the curses by utilising suggestions like those given above.

In any case, it is unreliable to build an interpretation of scripture upon a speculative eschatology.

Chapter Six

PILGRIMS AND PROPHECIES

SONGS OF ASCENTS

Fifteen Psalms (120-134) carry the title *Songs of Ascents* -

- ♦ **THE TITLE**
  - **A MYSTERY**

    No one is quite sure what this title means, but here are a number of common opinions -

    The word ascents means literally a going-up; hence it is thought that these Psalms may have been grouped for singing by pilgrims as they climbed up toward Jerusalem on their way to attend one of the great annual festivals (cp. Ps 122; and Is 30:29). One scholar, for example, translates the title as Songs of the Pilgrim Caravans.

    Similarly, it is suggested that they may have been composed, or sung, during the return of the Jews from their exile in Babylon (cp. Ps 126; and see also Ezr 7:9, where the same Hebrew word for *ascents* is used of the journey of the exiles from Babylon to Jerusalem.)

    Some argue that they were composed, or collected, for use by the temple choir as the choristers stood on the steps leading up to the great altar. There were 15 songs, to correspond to the 15 steps mentioned in Ezekiel's vision of the Ideal Temple (Ez 40:22,37). A similar idea is found in the Mishnah, which records that 15 steps led up from the Court of the Women to the Court of the Israelites "corresponding to the 15 Songs of Ascents in the Psalms, and upon them the Levites used to sing".

However, scholars have not been able to find any certain record that these were the Psalms they sang.

The word ascents may refer to the internal structure of these Psalms - that is, they are built up of thoughts that gradually ascend toward a climax (cp. 121, 123). However, such a structure is not apparent in all of these Psalms, and there are other Psalms not included in the group which more obviously contain a pattern of each succeeding verse being built upon an idea in the previous verses. So this suggestion remains more ingenious than probable.

Others claim that it is a musical term whose meaning is now entirely lost; or perhaps it refers to some facet of the poetic structure of these Psalms that we have not yet been able to identify. But they may have been songs for the ascending, that is, the treble or tenor, choir; or, they were songs written to be sung in progressively higher musical keys or settings.

An interesting though curious suggestion is that they celebrate that extraordinary occasion in the life of Hezekiah when he was given the sign of the shadow receding 10 degrees. This miracle was a guarantee from God that the king would live another 15 years (see 2 Kg 20:1-11; Is 38:1-10), which years, of course, are thought to match the 15 Psalms. Also, the Hebrew word translated steps in the story of the shadow is the same as that used in the title of our Psalms.

In additional support of this view, it is argued that

> the shadow receded 10 degrees and 10 of the 15 Psalms are anonymous;
>
> it could well be that Hezekiah was actually the author of those 10, especially since he was one of the most godly of Judah's kings (2 Kg 18:5-7);
>
> he was a known psalm-writer (Is 38:9-20), and he refers to songs of his that were used in the temple

liturgy (note vs. 20, *"we will sing **my** songs with **my** stringed instruments,"* lit.);

he was a great admirer of David, and sought to restore David's institutions (see 2 Ch 29:25-30; and cp. the references to David in the anonymous *Psalm 132*, which, some have suggested, may be the work of Hezekiah).

In fact, through his work of collecting, arranging, and transmitting the Old Testament scriptures, King Hezekiah had a great hand in preserving them for posterity (cp. 2 Ch 29:1-11; 31:20-21; Pr 25:1). Indeed, had it not been for Hezekiah's work, the upheavals, wars, and captivities that were shortly to overwhelm Judah may easily have resulted in the loss of the Hebrew scriptures. Thus he is a man of great importance in world history, and we all owe him a vast debt!

Perhaps much of that great work was done during those additional 15 years granted to him by God; and if that is so, and if he was in fact the compiler or composer of the *Songs of Ascents*, then those 15 Psalms take on a still deeper meaning.

You would find it an interesting project to study the records of Hezekiah's life, and to relate those 15 Psalms to the various events that happened to him (see 2 Kg 18-20, and 2 Ch 29-32). Some of the commentaries present ingenious attempts to make such an alignment.

♦ ARRANGEMENT

The *Songs of Ascents* are a miniature Psalter. They contain most of the themes of the larger collection. Also, like the whole Psalter, they are broken into five groups (each with three Psalms); and they are terminated by a doxology (134).

In each of those 5 segments of 3 Psalms, two of the songs are anonymous (perhaps composed by Hezekiah?), and one is either by David or Solomon. J. Sidlow Baxter adds that, "In each trio, the first Psalm is one of *trouble*, the second, one of *trust*, and the third, one of *triumph*." However, that analysis seems rather trite; so a more reasonable division would be as follows:

the first trio (120-122) focuses upon distress being met by faith, which finds its life and expression in the House of God;

the second trio (123-125) focuses upon the nation gaining stability and strength from its faithful worship of God and obedience to his laws;

the third trio (126-128) focuses upon home and family life;

the fourth trio (129-131) focuses upon the personal devotional life of the psalmist;

the fifth trio (132-134) focuses upon God's covenant with Israel and with the House of David, and upon the happiness of the people who yield to God's divine choice and upon whom his blessing has been commanded.

THE MESSIANIC PSALMS

♦ ABOUT THE ANOINTED ONE

The *Messianic Psalms* are not located in a single group (such as *The Songs of Ascents*), but they nonetheless form a specific body of Psalms within the Psalter. Why are they called *Messianic Psalms*? The name comes from a Hebrew word that means *Anointed*, and it is exactly equivalent to the Greek word from which we derive *Christ*. Hence these Psalms are all linked in some way with Jesus our Lord.

The Psalter is full of Christ. Jesus himself affirmed that the Psalms spoke of him (Lu 24:44; 20:41-42). According to some commentators there are more than 400 quotations from or allusions to the Psalms in the NT. Some Psalms are specifically identified in the NT as prophecies of Christ; in others, Christ may be found by inference, type, example, or analogy.

Opinions differ as to how many Psalms may be specifically called *messianic*, but the number seems to be about 15, namely, *Psalms 2, 8, 16, 22, 40, 45, 68, 69, 72, 89, 97, 102, 109, 110, 132*. In addition, single statements from various other Psalms are applied in the NT to Christ.

- **PRINCE, PRIEST, & PROPHET**
  - **AN IMPORTANT TITLE**

    The appellation *messiah* was applied by the Hebrews to three groups of people:

    ### KINGS

    The *kings* of Israel were called *messiahs*, that is, *anointed* by God (89:38,51), and they were in fact appointed to office by a ceremony of *anointing* with oil (1 Sa 10:1; 16:13; etc.)

    ### PRIESTS

    The title of *messiah* was also applied to members of the *priesthood*, for they shared in the anointing that was placed upon their forefather Aaron (Ex 29:7,21), and like him, had to be anointed with oil for service in the sanctuary (Ex 30:30-33).

    ### PROPHETS

    The true *prophets* were called *messiahs*, and the people were warned against committing sacrilege upon them (Ps 105:15).

    Those three groups provide us with a convenient way to study the messianic Psalms, for in those Psalms Christ is portrayed either as *Prince, Priest, or Prophet*; in him all three offices are marvelously combined -

  - **A GREAT REDEEMER**

  ### THE PRINCE OF ISRAEL

  Scattered throughout the Psalter is a group of diverse Psalms called *Royal Psalms*, which in one way or another deal with Israel's king:

  coronation odes addressed to the king (2, 72, 110)

  prayers for the king (20,61), or by the king (18, 28, 63, 101)

  hymns of praise by or for the king (21, 144)

a royal processional song (132)

a bridal ode for a royal marriage (45)

a meditation by the king (8)

a prayer for use by the king (89).

Those Psalms are all

> "ancient poems dating from the time of the monarchy and reflecting the idiom and ceremonial of the court. They concerned a king of their own period ... (who is) said to be son of God, his reign to be endless and stretching to the ends of the earth; he is to make peace and justice triumph and to be the saviour of his people. These expressions may seem extravagant, but they do not go beyond what other neighbouring people said of their sovereign and what Israel hoped of hers."[64]

The odes composed by modern poets laureate[65] are similar in scope and intention to Israel's *Royal Psalms*. For example, here is part of the Ode that Alfred Tennyson wrote to Queen Victoria in March 1851, shortly after his appointment as laureate -

Revered, beloved - O you that hold

A nobler office upon earth

Than arms, or power of brain or birth

Could give the warrior kings of old,

---

[64] New Jerusalem Bible, "Introduction to the Psalms."

[65] "Poet Laureate" is an "English title conferred by the crown on a poet whose duty it is to write commemorative verse. It is an outgrowth of medieval custom and later royal patronage of poets. Ben Jonson had what amounted to a laureateship, but Dryden, in 1670, was the first given the title. Among later laureates have been Wordsworth (1843-50), Tennyson (1850-92), and JohnMasefield (1930-67)." (The Concise Columbia Encyclopaedia).

> Victoria - since your Royal grace
> To one of less desert allows
> This laurel greener from the brows
> Of him that utter'd nothing base;
>
> . . . .
>
> Take, Madam, this poor book of song;
> For tho' the faults were thick as dust
> In vacant chambers, I could trust
> Your kindness. May you rule us long![66]

But Israel's coronation odes are very different from their modern counterparts, because in Israel the king was also the *anointed of the Lord*, and he ruled specifically and only as Yahweh's representative, who alone remained the true monarch of the nation. That religious dimension made Israel's monarchy unique in the ancient world, and gave a cast to the Psalms that set them apart from the royal odes composed by Israel's neighbours. Therefore always in the Psalms there is a sense that since none of the sons of David had fulfilled the ideal of messianic kingship, one day the Lord would send such a ruler, who would at last fulfil all the prayers of the people.

That explains also why the *Royal Psalms* were able to survive the devastations of the exile and the collapse of the monarchy. Why else would the scribes, once the monarchy had been destroyed, keep the royal Psalms in the Psalter? They did so because they recognised that the language employed in those Psalms transcended any of the previous kings and pointed to Another who was yet to come.

For us, that dream has been fulfilled in Christ, the ultimate *Royal Messiah*. Thus in **Psalm 2** we see Christ established upon the throne despite the hatred of the nations, while God declares

---

[66] Stanzas 1, 2, & 5. (The Ode has 9 stanzas.)

his Sonship and demands that all should submit to his dominion. Although this Psalm was probably used originally as a coronation ode for one of Israel's monarchs, its universal sweep lifts it far beyond acceptable courtly rhetoric. True, the kings of Israel were described as "sons" of God (2 Sa 7:14), but there is a grandeur about *this* Son that could never be ascribed to any of those sadly inadequate rulers!

Against that background, the term *Messiah* is first introduced into the Psalter in *Psalm 2:2*, and the prophecy is made that his Father will give him as his inheritance the ends of the earth.

Similarly, the following Psalms probably all had orginally only local significance, and were connected with some specific royal event in Israel, but it became impossible to limit them to an earthly monarch. The language used, the ideas expressed, the drama described, all point toward that one Great King in whom all the ideals of God's *Messiah* would come to their final focus and fulfilment:

> in **Psalm 8** he is the ideal Man, destined to reign over all things, and to demonstrate in himself the high calling and authority that the human race should have, but failed to fulfil (He 2:5-11).
>
> in **Psalm 45** he is the Royal Bridegroom, taking to himself the Princess, his Bride - which for us is a picture of the union between Christ and the Church, and of the *"marriage supper of the Lamb"* (Re 19:6-9).
>
> in **Psalm 72** we find a marvellous prophecy of the peace, prosperity, and limitless beauty of his eternal kingdom
>
>> what a joyous day it will be when this King assumes his earthly dominion!
>>
>> in ancient Israel, the furthest reach of empire was the banks of the Euphrates; but this King will extend his authority "from the River, to the ends of the earth" (vs. 8).
>
> in **Psalms 89 & 132** God swears by his own unbreakable oath (89:3; 132:11) that the dominion of his Anointed King will remain secure forever, and that his empire will

> expand across the endless ages (89:4,28-29,35-37; 132:17-18)
>
>> though David and his lineage were called God's "anointed ones" (messiahs, 89:20,51; 132:10), it was never supposed that these promises could truly be fulfilled in one of those men
>>
>> from the earliest times it was realised that Another would have to come, both of, yet not of, David, in whom alone the word of God could be fulfilled.
>>
>> in *Psalm 110* the revelation of God's Ideal Monarch reaches its apogee.
>>
>> the kings of Israel had been called
>>
>>> "the breath of our nostrils, the Lord's anointed" (La 4:20, which was spoken of the pitiful Zedekiah), and
>>>
>>> "the lamp of Israel" *(2 Sa 21:17), and*
>>>
>>> "the shield of the people" *(Ps 84:9; 89:18), and*
>>>
>>> they were even described in terms of sonship and co-regency with God *(Psalm 2).*

With a little stretch of imagination, and by a permissible royal flattery, it was possible to apply such expressions to faulty monarchs - although the promises did continue to demand a better and greater fulfilment. But in *Psalm 110* the language breaks through all natural barriers. No mere son of man can fulfil such demands. We are now in the presence of the Son of God!

Even if this Psalm was originally used as an enthronement song, celebrating the crowning of a new king, and expressing a pious hope for a glorious reign, the people must have realised that only in a figurative or partial sense could its terminology be applied to an earthly monarch. The apostles certainly understood the Psalm in that way, and made it the most-quoted piece of the Old Testament, for it is either quoted or alluded to some 25 times in the New Testament. In *verse one* alone the apostles saw the ***deity*** of Christ (Lu 20:42-43), his ***ascension*** to the Father's right hand (Ro 8:34; Ac 2:34-35; He 1:3), and his everlasting *sovereignty* (1 Co 15:25).

But *Psalm 110* goes beyond the *kingship* of Christ, and declares also his undying *priesthood* ....

THE PRIEST OF ISRAEL

Psalm 110:4 says of Christ, *"you are a priest forever, after the order of Melchizedek."* The analogy refers back to that mysterious figure in Ge 14:18 ff., who is the archetypal priest-king:

> "(The) relevance of every detail of that narrative to the high-priesthood of Christ is expounded in Hebrews 7, which itself leads on to the fuller discussion of priesthood and sacrifice in Hebrews 8-10. So the single sentence in Psalm 110, which is quoted in Hebrews 5:6, is the germ of one of the great themes of that epistle, and consequently the means of showing how the earthly priesthood of the Old Testament was destined to be superseded by the heavenly priesthood of Christ. Our understanding of the relationship of the old order to the new would have been unimaginably poorer without this verse and its exposition"[67]

That old priestly ministry had two major aspects -

Sacrifice

The first responsibility of a priest was to stand at the altar, between the Holy God and corrupt man, and to make a sacrifice for sin. In Christ, priest and victim were combined; he was both the offering and the offerer.

---

[67] Tyndale Old Testament Commentary, "Psalms 1-72"; by Derek Kidner; Inter-Varsity Press, London, 1973; pg. 23.

Nine of the Psalms are reckoned either to predict or to illustrate the passion of Christ - *2, 16, 22, 40, 41, 55, 69, 102, 109*. Out of those nine, *Psalm 69* provided for the apostles more verses relating to the mission and sufferings of Christ than any other passage of scripture –

69:4	Jn 15:25
69:9	Jn 2:17; Ro 15:3
69:21	Mt 27:34,48; Mk 15:23,36; Lu 23:36; Jn 19:29
69:22-23	Ro 11:9-10
69:24	Re 16:1
69:25	Ac 1:20
69:28	Ph 4:3; Re 3:5; 13:8; 17:8; 20:12,15; 21:27.

The greatest detail concerning the cross is found in the first half of *Psalm 22* -

vs. 1	- his cry from the cross (Mt 27:46)
vs. 6,7	- the mockery of the crowd (Mt 27:39)
vs. 8	- the taunts they made (Mt 27:43)
vs. 14	- his dislocated joints (Jn 19:18)
vs. 15	- the thirst he endured (Jn 19:28)
vs. 16	- his crucifixion (Jn 19:18; 20:25)
vs. 17	- the effect of the lash (Jn 19:1)
vs. 18	- the lottery for his garments (Mt 27:35)

Thus Christ presented himself to Israel, and to the world, as the Lamb of God, making atonement for the sins of all mankind. In this act, he was both officiating *Priest* and expiating *Victim*. But was he just another religious martyr? Can we be sure his death has value for all who believe? Yes! For the grave could not hold him (Ps 16:8-11), and he ascended back to heaven's right hand (68:18; 118:22-24; and cp 24:7-10).

Intercession

The second great task of a priest is to make *intercession* before God on behalf of others. This aspect of the priestly work of Christ is not stressed in the Psalms, except by extension from his identification with Melchizedek (see He 7:15-25).

The priesthood is also implicit in the *humanity* of Christ (for every true priest is taken from among the very people he is to serve, He 2:10-11) and the apostles saw in the Psalms numerous examples of this. The best of those is found in *Hebrews 2*, which quotes *Psalms 8:4-6; 22:22; 18:2*; and by those references demonstrates, not only that the Messiah was a true man, but that he *had* to be one in order to fulfil his messianic office -

> *"Since the people have flesh and blood, he too had to share in their humanity so that by his death he might destroy the one who holds the power of death ... That is why he had to be made like his companions in every way, so that he might become a merciful and faithful high priest in the service of God ... " (He 2:14,17).*

A further indication of the priestly ministry of Christ may be seen in the portrayal of the Good Shepherd in Psalm 23:1-6.

The Prophet of Israel

The Suffering Servant of God in the first half of Psalm 22 becomes, in the second half, the Prophetic Oracle of God. He begins in vs. 22, 25 -

> "I will declare your name to my companions; in the gathering of the people I will worship you ... You draw praise from me in the great congregation, and in the presence of those who fear you I will honour my vows."

then follow the declarations of his universal triumph and the spread of righteousness among all peoples.

Once it is allowed that in such verses, behind the voice of the Psalmist, the voice of Christ the Prophet of God is heard, then his accent can be discovered in numerous other places in the Psalter. Wherever the victory of the Kingdom of God and of the servants of God is predicted, there the Prophet speaks. A notable example (which is applied to Christ in the NT) can be found in Psalm 40:6-10.

♦ THE SON OF GOD

The Psalter not only affirms that Christ is Prophet, Priest, and King, but also plainly declares his **deity**

"Thy throne, O God, is for ever and ever." (45:6)

Despite the startling implications of that statement, it was faithfully preserved in both the Hebrew and Greek versions of the OT. For Christians, its meaning is put beyond doubt by Hebrews 1:8, *which boldly contrasts this way of addressing the Son with the manner of addressing angels.*

> "(This) is perhaps the boldest Messianic oracle in the Psalter; but it is not alone. The same chapter of Hebrews finds references to Christ in two other sayings that speak immediately of God. One of these is Psalm 97:7 ("all the gods bow down before him") ... (the other) is Psalm 102:25-27, which is quoted in He 1:10-12 as God's address to One whom he entitles 'Lord', and to whom he ascribes eternity and the creating of the universe ... So startling an exegesis of the Psalm must have been too dazzling to contemplate, until events, in the coming of Christ, accustomed the eyes of believers to the full glory of the truth"[68]

Christ may also be seen as the Son of God *in* Psalm 2:7,12; 110:1-3.

---

[68] Ibid. pg. 21.

2.4 A FINAL GROUP

Let us close this section on the Messianic Psalms with a final group of Psalms, 22, 23, 24. These three belong together, and together they give a magnificent picture of Christ as

> The Grieving Saviour
>
> The Gentle Shepherd
>
> The Glorious Sovereign.

There we see the Cross, the Crook, and the Crown. Also, as J Sidlow Baxter points out, these three Psalms

> "strikingly correspond with the three outstanding NT references to our Lord's 'shepherd' work. In John 10 he is the 'good' Shepherd who gives his life for the sheep (as in Psalm 22). In Hebrews 13:20-21 he is the 'great' Shepherd who, being brought again from the dead, perfects that which concerns his flock (as in Psalm 23). In 1 Peter 5:4 he is the 'chief' Shepherd who is to appear in glory, bringing crowns of reward (matching Psalm 24)."

OTHER GROUPS OF PSALMS

♦ PRAYERS FOR MORNING AND EVENING

Psalm 3, for morning and evening

Psalm 4, for the evening

Psalm 5, for the morning.

♦ THREE ANTHEMS OF PRAISE

Three Psalms are linked together by a strong Hebrew adverb, m'ohd, *which means* greatly *or* exceedingly:

Psalm 46 celebrates Israel's deliverance from peril (vs. 1, God greatly helps us)

Psalm 47 extols the power and majesty of God, the Saviour of his people (vs. 9, God is greatly exalted)

Psalm 48 portrays the glory of the City God has marvelously preserved (vs. 1, God is greatly to be praised).

♦ TWO PSALMS OF TRUST

Psalms 90 & 91 *can be taken together as a comment on* Deuteronomy 33:27, "The eternal God is your refuge, and underneath are the everlasting arms." *They may both have been composed by Moses:*

Psalm 90, *which reflects,* "The eternal God is your refuge"

Psalm 91, *which reflects,* "Underneath are the everlasting arms."

♦ A GROUP OF CHORAL CANTATAS

Psalm 95-100 comprise six liturgical songs that were probably sung together, perhaps antiphonally, as a magnificent anthem of praise (similar to the succession of songs in a modern oratorio, such as Handel's Messiah). The central theme of each of these Psalms is, "The Lord reigns!" (97:1; 99:1)

♦ TWO CREATION HYMNS

Psalms 103 & 104 comprise a double anthem of praise to God as creator of man and of all the earth. Each poem begins and ends with the same refrain: "Praise the Lord, O my soul!"

> (Note: the final "Praise the Lord!" in Psalm 104 almost certainly should be placed at the beginning of Psalm 105, to match the ending shout of that Psalm, and the beginning and ending shouts of Psalm 106. Those two Psalms then comprise a fine doxology, marking the end of Book IV of the Psalter.)

♦ THE GREAT HALLEL

Psalms 113 - 118 and 136 were called the "Hallel" ("Praise") by the Jews, with Psalm 136 being known as the "Great Hallel."

It was mandatory to sing the Hallel at each of the major annual feasts (Passover, Pentecost, and Tabernacles), and especially at the Passover, where the Hallel was divided into two parts:

the first (113 - 114), which was sung before the meal; and

the second (115 - 118), which was sung after the meal.

This is the *"hymn"* mentioned in *Matthew 26:30*. The disciples did not fully understand what they were singing, but the words of *Psalm 118:21-25* must have had a profound significance for Jesus (cp. Mt 21:42). The disciples and Jesus would all have been able to recite or sing the *Hallel* from memory, since early in his life every Jewish boy was expected to learn fully each of the *Hallel* Psalms.

John 7:37-39 is also connected with the Hallel. The events described in that passage occurred when Jesus went to Jerusalem to celebrate the feast of Tabernacles (Le 23:39-43). On the last day of the feast, the "greatest" day (vs. 37), it was customary for a priest to carry a golden pitcher down to the Pool of Siloam and to fill it with water. The pitcher was then carried back through the city to the temple, while the thronging procession sang, "With joy you will draw water from the wells of salvation!" (Is 12:3). When the priest came to the temple altar, the water was poured out as a special offering to God, signifying thanksgiving for the rain that had fallen in the past season, and a prayer that the next season would be abundantly fruitful.

While this ceremony was being performed, the huge congregation, along with the temple choirs and musicians, sang the Hallel, coming to a thrilling three-fold climax at vs. 1, 25, & 29 of Psalm 118, when they would all pause and raise a tremendous shout of praise to God. Against that background Jesus "stood up and cried aloud, 'Is any of you thirsty? Then come to me and drink ... A river of living water shall flow from within you!'" He was, of course, referring to Holy Spirit baptism (vs. 39), in which he plainly saw a fulfilment of the typology of Tabernacles. The Feast of Tabernacles celebrated

>Israel's deliverance from Egypt;

>the ingathering of the harvest;

>the future restoration of Israel in the Kingdom.

In us, as shown by the words of Jesus, those three things are realised when we receive the gift of the Holy Spirit.

♦ DOXOLOGY

As I have already noted, the Psalter concludes with a lengthy doxology, comprising *Psalms 146 - 150,* which were perhaps composed by the final compiler of the collection, the person who gathered together the five

Books as we now have them. The same editor/compiler may also have composed the anonymous *Psalm 1*, to serve as an introduction to his collection. The five Psalms in the doxology may have been intended to represent each of the five Books of the Psalter.

So we come to the end of this brief survey of the Psalms of Israel. My intention has been threefold:

>**first**, to highlight certain aspects of the Psalms, sufficient, I hope, to open your eyes to the immense wealth of material that lies there, waiting to be explored;

>**second**, to encourage you to start reading some of the far more detailed Introductions that can be found in the various commentaries, and also to inspire you to give more attention to individual Psalms; and

>**third**, to provide a foundation for the second part of this book by conveying a picture of the richness, skill, and diversity of Israel's worship experience.

Let us then, without further delay, embark on our study of Christian worship.

Part Two

AT THE THRONE OF GRACE

Preface

THE WORSHIP LEADER

Hippocrates, the father of all physicians, once said that "prayer is indeed good; but while calling on God, a man should himself lend a hand." This book is devoted to the second part of that proposition, which here means that public worship cannot be built upon spiritual impulses alone. Good worship requires good preparation and often also the hand of a skilled worship leader. Why is that so? People are often content to expend the lowest input of spiritual energy their leaders will allow. They can become satisfied with the role of spectators watching a group of professionals perform at the altar or on the platform. Sometimes, if they do happen to break out of lethargy and conceive a passion to worship God with enthusiasm, they become impatient with *any* leadership, and demand the right to express themselves in whatever way they please.

The first fault leads to an arid formalism; the second to a crass emotionalism. Against those, our goal should be to worship God both in spirit and in truth, with grace and order as well as with life and liberty (Jn 4:23; 1 Co 14:40). Like Aaron of old, when we come before the Lord God we should be clothed equally with the *beauty* of dignity, and the *glory* of vitality (Ex 28:2). Usually, corporate worship best achieves that balanced character when it is directed by a gifted worship leader. What does that mean? It describes a person who is skilled in two things:

- ♦ an ability to elicit from the people the highest response they can give;
- ♦ an ability to hold that response within the bounds of dignity.

Where there is a lack of such leadership something (or someone) else may rise up to take command. For example, the crowd itself may take control, which is a sure way to chaos. Or perhaps the musicians (who should always be under direction) may seize the initiative. But be sure of this: create a vacuum, and the wrong thing will usually fill it!

The better way is for a gifted worship leader to be in charge, one who can draw the people to worship God not just with all their *heart*, but also with all their *mind*. Such a leader will not allow worship to become perfunctory, but neither will he or she permit it to become formless. Under proper direction worship remains disciplined, yet throbbing with divine life. The worship thus created has liberty, but not license; it is passionate and powerful, yet also graceful and purposeful.

Because of the role of the worship leader in helping to create fine worship, I have chosen to begin my study with that role, which many readers may think is an unusual place to start. Most books on the subject, I suppose, would begin with something more theological. But I want this study to be not only instructive, but also practical.

The best worship leaders are born to the task. They have just the right mix of personality, manner, voice, and spiritual endowments to give them an almost irresistible influence over a congregation. Seemingly without effort, they can arouse from a listless crowd a mighty chorus of praise and adoration. Yet even men and women of average competence can successfully lead worship if they observe a few basic rules. The pages that follow are an attempt to set out some of those rules, along with a discussion of various aspects of worship in the church.[69]

I once heard it said, *"When giants are mentioned in the Bible they are always on the side of the enemy."* That may not be quite true, for Paul declared that God does call a few who are powerful, wise, and noble (1 Co 1:26). Yet it remains clear that God more often chooses what is *foolish in the world to shame the wise, and what is weak in the world to shame the strong ... so that no human being can boast in the presence of God* (1 Co 1:27-29). Even the feeblest among us can hope to do something good for God (Zc 12:8) if we put together a reasonable mixture of wisdom, divine grace, know-how, and the quickening of the Holy Spirit!

But what if you are not and never will be a worship leader? Only the chapter that follows this *Preface* concentrates on that worthy individual, the remaining chapters deal with more sparkling facets of the jewel of praise. Nonetheless, there are qualities a worship leader should have that should

---

[69] I have written a companion booklet to this manual, called "The Worship Leader". It provides practical instruction on platform and music technique.

equally be the possession of every Christian, so you will still find the chapter useful. Further, you ought to know what a worship leader should be, so that you have some criteria by which to measure those who serve (or want to serve) your church in that capacity.

Please do not blame me for not achieving what I have not attempted. You will search these pages in vain for a comprehensive doctrine of worship. You will not even find a serious definition of the word *worship*. That broad term has been used in different ways by many people. One writer will restrict its use to private devotions, another to public service, another to a solemn liturgy, or another to non-liturgical praise. In these pages I am using *worship* as an inclusive term to describe those corporate acts of prayer and praise, of scripture reading and testimony, that Christians perform when they assemble in the name of Christ - whether in a church, a house, or a rented hall.

The cartoons were drawn by Australian artist and pastor, *Wayne Vincent*.

Chapter Seven

PERSONAL MOTIVATION

Keith Ewing writes,

> "Sometimes we Pentecostals leave a worship service with a numbing sense that it was inadequate. We sense that we have failed to participate in true worship, and this we compound with guilt and frustration. How did we miss getting with the flow of a meeting seemingly enjoyed by others? Are we unwittingly responsible? Are we contributing to our own spiritual demise? Or had the worship service itself been contaminated by alien influences?"[70]

He suggests some reasons for this state (which I have summarised):

- worship has decayed into a "theatrical performance" of songs and sermons by professional performers, who attract applause to themselves instead of directing praise toward God.[71]

- a worship style has been adopted that "exploits sentiment" and lacks integrity because it depends on artificially stimulated emotion.

- the worship fails to satisfy because it is "all style and no content"; the people have been "manipulated by leaders pretending to be blessed" in their staged antics.

---

[70] From an article in "Agora" magazine, date and issue number unknown to me.
[71] See Addendum on "Applause".

♦ a contrived spiritual "high" has been produced by urging the people to ever-more-boisterous praise; or their emotions have been worked on by numerous repetitions of a song.

I have myself observed all those and worse in various meetings. Sadly, the people were willing victims. A friend of mine once told me how the congregation in an enthusiastic and rowdy church shouted with excitement every time he slapped at some mosquitoes. He was mystified by their cries, until he discovered later that they saw his slaps as a sign that *"he had got the glory"*!

No doubt that is an extreme example; but it does show how people can be manipulated into a certain response. Yet wise, responsible and godly leadership can overcome all those follies, those sorry betrayals of true worship. That premise underlies this chapter: the role of the worship leader is imperative if the people of God are to be drawn into a worship experience that highly exalts God and deeply satisfies the worshippers.

A precedent for the role of worship leader was set by the cantor in ancient Israel. It was his task to direct the great choir, the orchestra, and the vast congregation in praising the God of Israel (compare Ne 12:46; plus references in the Psalm inscriptions and elsewhere to *"the chief musician"*). Some form of responsive singing was evidently also common in Israel - notice *Psalm 124:1; 129:1*; perhaps also *118:1-4*; and *Psalm 136*. In fact, any study of the worship of ancient Israel quickly shows it was a combination of exuberant spontaneity and disciplined liturgy. There was form, and there was freedom.

A similar mix still seems to be the best way to structure the kind of worship that involves the whole person, body, soul, and spirit. So the wise worship leader will strive to create a blend of control and liberty, guiding the people into worshipping God, with *understanding* and with *spirit* (1 Co 14:15).

In charismatic/pentecostal services the worship leader may occupy the platform for as long as (or even longer than) the preacher. The leader's role is crucial in preparing the people for the coming ministry of the Word. If the leader performs his task well, the people will be ready to hear the Word with joy. If the leader fails, then the preacher himself may have to spend time trying to prepare the congregation to receive his message.

The task of leading a meeting, then, should be seen as a definite ministry, and it should be approached with the same prayer, faith, and dedication that is expected of the preacher. Because so few leaders can be found who take that kind of responsible attitude, many preachers prefer to lead their own meetings. Only then can they be sure the people will be prepared, through the right kind of praise and worship, to yield to the Word of God. Yet it is often better for the first part of a meeting to be taken by someone other than the preacher; and most preachers are happy to surrender that ministry to another competent person, if one is available.

Then again, a good preacher is not necessarily a good worship leader. A competent leader may be able to prepare the meeting better than the preacher could for himself. In that situation everybody benefits - the congregation, the preacher, and, of course, the worship leader who has found an important and fulfilling ministry.

There is hardly any joy so great as knowing you have successfully taken hold of a diverse group of people, moulded them into a worshipping community, and now you are standing with them at the pinnacle of inspired and exalted praise.

Many preachers prefer to lead their own meetings.

You can begin to experience that joy by confronting the theme of this chapter: *the worship leader's motivation*. There are worship leaders who perform well, but whose motives are wrong, which make them little more than *clanging gongs* (1 Co 13:1). Possession of the right kind of objective will outweigh many other inadequacies. *"Love,"* it is said, *"covers a multitude of sins!"* Hence the chief motivation of any worship leader should be -

THE GLORY OF GOD

According to the Greek legend, one of the mighty warriors at Troy was an Ethiopian monarch named Memnon. He was black as smooth ebony, and was said to be the handsomest man alive. He fought with the Trojans against the Greeks, and slaughtered many of them. However, one day he fell into combat with Achilles, the most renowned of the Greek heroes, and after an awful struggle was slain by him.

Strangely, Memnon's name became associated with divinely inspired song. It was said that the warrior's female slaves mourned his death so bitterly that Zeus turned them into birds called Memnonides who returned to his tomb each year to offer their heaven-born laments. Centuries later this story was linked with a huge black statue that stood at Egyptian Thebes, and was thought to represent the Trojan hero. Every morning at dawn plaintive melodies, like the songs of the memnonides, issued from its open mouth and made the stone goliath famous throughout the ancient world. It was known everywhere as the Singing Statue. Historians now suppose the heat of the rising sun warmed the hollow stone, thus causing the air to rush out of its narrow throat with an organ-like effect.

Just as that lifeless sculpture produced seemingly divine music when it was struck by the light of the sun, so do we need the touch of the Holy Spirit to turn our dead words into a divine anthem. True worship cannot exist unless it is in-breathed by God. The actions of worship, unless they are enlivened by the Holy Spirit, remain empty husks, hollow sounds.

But the Father does not inspire worship that has the praise of man as its real goal. That is why worship leaders must strive to exalt Christ and to glorify God; they should depend upon the Holy Spirit to work with them and to draw the people into the holiest courts of praise.

You had better realise this at once: if your chief reason for taking leadership is to gratify yourself, to feed your own pride, the people will quickly penetrate your sham. Nothing is so easily recognised on a platform as an ego trip. Just a few minutes will be enough to make the people aware that something false is being projected; the Spirit of Christ within them always reacts with distaste against any kind of carnal spirit.

Many preachers prefer to lead their own meetings

The antidote to such self-aggrandisement is to prepare for your task with earnest prayer, making yourself wholly dependent upon God, and setting yourself to do nothing except for the glory of God. It is difficult to be proud if you have heartily confessed your helplessness and have vowed to exalt Christ. You must yourself be a true worshipper before you can lead other people in worship.

Don't Be Too Humble!

Don't let your desire to be rid of all wrong motives turn itself into a problem. Some people bring themselves into bondage by becoming too intent upon having nothing but perfect motives. You should refrain from taking either your pride or your humility too seriously.

The fact is, no matter how hard you try, your motives will always be mixed. You cannot feel as humble as you would like. You cannot be wholly rid of pride. You would probably be impossible to live with if you ever did achieve such "perfection". So be content to be as sincere as you can (without trying too desperately), and learn how to live cheerfully with an imperfect humility, and with a residue of pride.

An excess of seriousness is a pestilence that plagues many devout Christians.

If you cannot live with yourself with good humour it is unlikely you will be happy with anyone else! So do not become one of those discontented, morose, and sombre perfectionists. Such people are not very welcome on the public platform - indeed, they are hardly welcome anywhere!

An over-serious Christian is also a prime candidate for personal breakdown. One of my unhappiest experiences occurred when I met in a corridor a pastor who responded to my friendly greeting by bursting into convulsive and anguished sobs. He wept bitterly while I stood there in dismay, for I had always imagined him a strong and upright man of God. But he was too earnest. Every mistake was a crisis, every failure a tragedy. At the moment of our meeting the pressure of it all broke him to pieces. He had to go back to secular work for several years, but was eventually restored to the ministry with a more realistic attitude about himself.

Now a final word on being motivated by the glory of God -

> "Worship is man's foremost duty and his greatest privilege. In worship man makes two affirmations: he affirms the existence of a being higher than himself, and he affirms his own capacity for worship. In brief, worship is an affirmation of God and of self.

> "The person who worships God will not exclaim with Swinburne, 'Glory to man in the highest!' Nor will he agree with Stevenson's description of man as a mere 'disease of agglutinated dust'.

> "Rather, in worship, man gives recognition to the 'worthship' of God as creator and redeemer, and to his own 'worthship' as creature and object of redemption."[72]

So the good worship leader will display these two characteristics: a true sense of *God*; and a true sense of *himself*. Which takes us on to the second part of a proper motivation -

PREPARATION FOR THE WORD

One of the most powerful aspects of the latter-day outpouring of the Holy Spirit has been the restoration of scripture to its rightful place in the devotional lives of the people and in public worship. Prior to this outpouring preaching had fallen into bad favour. From thousands of pulpits, the people heard only pretty little homilies, and were content to have it so. That situation, of course, still prevails in many places. But where the breath of the Holy Spirit has brought new life, it has also brought a new thirst for the Word of God. That is important, for it needs to be recognised that worship is not an end in itself. The purpose of worship is to draw the people close to God so they might properly hear the word of God. If worship is allowed to become its own end it will soon lapse into a soulish emotionalism, becoming a means of personal pleasure, something to be enjoyed for its own sake, rather than a channel of divine glory.

That has sometimes happened in charismatic circles. People become so enamoured with worship that preaching is squeezed out of their programmes. The sternest part of worship is the discipline and spiritual maturity required to give earnest attention to the exposition of scripture. We dare not dispense with that essential component of true worship (Jn 4:23). So the leader's _primary_ task is to prepare the people (after they have spoken *to* God in worship) to be ready to hear *from* God through the Word. If this is so, then it would seem wise to discover beforehand the theme of the meeting, or of the message, and to structure the worship programme accordingly.

---

[72] From an article in "Christianity Today", September 14th, 1973; author's name unknown to me.

For example, if the preacher plans to bring a challenging call to holiness, it is discouraging for him to sit through a preliminary hour of cheerful, lightweight songs, mixed up with many jokes and other distractions. On another occasion, all of those preliminaries might have been quite appropriate. But on this occasion, the preacher will have to spend several minutes of his time creating a mood among the people that will make them more receptive to his message.

The leader's _secondary_ task is to draw the people to true worship, to motivate and inspire them, to help them to attain a height of worship, or a depth, that without him they would have found impossible to reach. Which raises an interesting question: what comprises true worship? Is it emotional, or free of emotion? Is it boisterous or quiet?

The best answer is: worship may embrace any of those things, yet it goes beyond all of them. What character worship should have at any given time depends, as I have suggested, on what purpose the church is seeking to achieve - whether a call to joy, or to weeping, or to praise, prayer, witness, holiness, or whatever may be the command of the Spirit.

The best way, if not the only way, to determine whether or not the people have fulfilled the call to worship God truly is to examine the *product* of their worship. In general, I have observed that *true* worship produces these four things:

Don't take your humility too seriously.

Don't Take your humility too seriously.

♦ AN ENCOUNTER WITH CHRIST

Although every believer has immediate entrance into the holiest by the blood of Jesus (He 10:19-20), there is still a need for us to draw near to God and collectively to seek the heavenly vision. Through worship Christ is unveiled. His glory is more vividly disclosed to the adoring heart. To those who stand in the house of the Lord the beauty of the King is revealed (Ps 27:4). As they come away from worship, the people should know they have seen the Lord.

♦ RENEWAL, NOT EXHAUSTION

When worship is informal, and the people have been brought to a pitch of joy and excitement, it is possible for the soul to gain ascendancy over the spirit, so that their worship becomes an emotional indulgence rather than a spiritual sacrifice (He 13:15). Revelry supplants devotion; personal exultation replaces divine exaltation. When that has happened, the people are likely to have a later reaction of emotional exhaustion. They will feel wearied, not refreshed, by their worship. True worship brings renewal (Is 40:31); it leaves the worshipper feeling alive, invigorated, and ready to serve God in strength! Not drained out, but filled up!

♦ LOVE FOR EACH OTHER

Worship that descends to the level of merely personal excitement, or becomes a means of personal gratification, creates self-centred worshippers. They make a show of praising God, but their real desire is towards themselves. Their own pleasure is their aim, not the pleasure of God; so they concentrate on themselves and become more isolated from their worshipping neighbours. By contrast, true worship creates love, for God and for neighbour. It removes hostilities, it builds unity, it produces harmony. As they leave the worship service the people will feel a deep bond with each other and with the Father in Christ.

♦ HUMILITY AND OBEDIENCE

If worship does not result in a sincere humility and in a more dedicated obedience to the will of God, then its genuineness should certainly be questioned.

Those four criteria provide a guide by which you can determine whether the worship programme has just been an emotional funfest, or a genuine act of praise, submission, and prayer. *Note*: I am not implying that worship cannot be exciting or enjoyable, nor that emotion must be removed from worship. God forbid!

True worship can hardly avoid being deeply emotional (Ps 42:7-8). It should bring indescribable joy (1 Pe 1:8). As the psalmist said:

> "Let the righteous be merry; let them exult in the presence of God; let them be jubilant with joy!" (Ps 68:3)

But all that emotion, that gladness, must be held within the boundaries of a truly spiritual outreach toward God. Thus Bernard Schalm suggests that true worship will produce four responses: *love, joy, confidence, submission*. All of those will be felt as part of the worship experience, and are indications that the worship is both moved by God and is directed toward God. Yet they can all become misdirected and carnal, so that

love may become merely a sensual emotion;

joy a purely soulish exuberance;

confidence a false trust in feelings alone; and

submission a bondage to man.

Part of the way to prevent such lapses, and to maintain a high quality in worship, is to keep the worshippers' attention fixed upon the Giver of the feelings rather than upon the feelings themselves. Worship should flow out of grateful recognition of the revelation of himself that God has given us in Christ. It should be founded upon the Word, not upon experiences, which are variable, but scripture remains unchanged for ever.

The grace and mercy God has bestowed upon us in Christ, as revealed in scripture, are more than adequate grounds for dedicated worship, whether or not there is an emotional reaction within us. The worship leader should constantly mingle the Word with his exhortations and keep Christ central.

LOVE FOR THE PEOPLE

Here is the third and simplest part of the worship leader's motivation. The first two parts (the glory of God, and preparation for the Word) are more elusive, more difficult to grip; but this is easily recognised, and easily fulfilled. You simply have to decide whether you are on the platform because you love yourself, or because you love the people of God. If *you* won't answer that question, the *people* will answer it for you; especially if they sense (as they quickly will) that you love yourself more than you love them.

All platform ministry should be motivated by a warm love for your audience. It should fill you with delight just to see the people assembled for worship. There should be something in you that reaches out to them with a yearning desire for their health and happiness (3 John 2). You should be longing to bring them pleasure, to lift them up, to ennoble their lives by helping them to enter into a total worship experience. If you have that kind of love, three things will follow (and indeed, will be a sign that you have it):

- **You will be continually aware of the people.**

You will not get lost in your own glory. You will be attentive to what the people are doing; you will know what is happening among them. You will not ignore the aged in favour of the young, nor the weak in favour of the strong, nor the shy in favour of the extroverts, nor the stranger in favour of the friend.

- **You will remain concerned about each individual.**

You will structure the programme so that all those who are present will feel they have a vital part to play. No one should feel as though he or she does not belong. If you truly love the people you will unconsciously convey to them an impression of deeply caring about them, and that you are sensitive to their needs, hurts, and desires. If you truly love them, you will neither pamper them nor bully them; you will just give them firm leadership in doing the will of God.

- **You will refuse to manipulate the people**

To the seven things Solomon said are an abomination to the Lord (Pr 6:16-19), I would like to add one more: *leaders and preachers who play games with people*. They make people in the congregation the butt of their jokes; they set people up for stunts; they exploit their reactions, they simulate religious prostration; they create an artificial *"falling under the power"*.

Either subtly or overtly these manipulators take away from men and women their God-given freedom to say *"No!"* They coerce people into acting against their own sense of what is right for them. In a variety of ways such leaders seek to enhance themselves at the expense of the dignity and well-being of God's children. They display a poor ethical standard. They are scandalous. Their behaviour is a betrayal of spiritual authority. It is inexcusable.

I do not object to humour at another's expense if it occurs naturally, and brings no embarrassment. Nor do I object to physical manifestations such as *"falling under the power"* if they are a genuine and voluntary response to the presence and influence of the Holy Spirit. But I do protest sternly against leaders who deliberately and callously *"use"* the people of God for their own aggrandisement, who make a big display of people falling down, who coerce their collapse, or even push them down and then pretend it was an act of God.

Unhappily, those leaders often do not realise what they are doing. They are merely following a practice that has proved "successful" (whether for themselves or other leaders), and they have never bothered to think about the propriety of their behaviour.

I beg you not to fall into the same error. Examine your platform ministry. Ask yourself **why** you are doing certain things - what is your goal, what is your motive, what is the result in the lives of the people and in their worship? Do nothing merely for the sake of doing it. Do nothing merely because it seems successful. The end does not justify the means if the means are unethical. Successful worship leading depends primarily on a right motivation. If you earnestly desire the glory of God, if you revere the preaching of the Word, if you genuinely love the people of God, you will already be well advanced in expertise!

Chapter Eight

PROFESSIONALS APPROVED

Once upon a time, according to a Greek myth, there were twin brothers named Amphion and Zethus who made themselves rulers of Thebes. The god Hermes gave a lyre to Amphion, who became much devoted to it and soon drew from it charming melodies. Zethus, however, gave himself to outdoor activities and became very strong. He mocked Amphion, calling him effeminate, while boasting of his own manly powers. But when they had to build a wall around the city, Amphion showed how mighty his music was by using the magic sounds of his lyre to pull the huge stones behind him and to lay them gently in place. That was a feat of strength that Zethus, with all of his vigour, could not equal. So Amphion became renowned as the man whose music fortified a great city.

That myth reflects a wide-spread belief in the ancient world that there is spiritual power in music. The gods gave music to man as a heavenly boon, and they were pleased when music was given back to them in melodious worship. Music, the ancients thought, subdued demons and attracted the strength and favour of heaven.

In a more noble fashion, the same ideas are taught in scripture. The psalmist, for example, was confident that a lovely song was more pleasing to God than a slaughtered ox (Ps 69:30-31). Indeed, we must admit that

> "music was God's idea - a luxurious gift to human beings, which has enriched our life since earliest times. In the Old Testament God welded music and worship, a glorious union still stable today. Of all the religions of the world, Christianity has contributed most to the great

music of the world. God takes music in the church seriously. But does anyone else in the church today?"[73]

Since you are reading this book I am sure you do take your church music seriously, and you want both to please God and to benefit the people by the use of music in worship. To do that requires proper recognition of three different kinds of musical expression: *"psalms, hymns, and spiritual songs"* (Ep 5:18-19; Cl 3:16). I may be exercising a little poetic license, but I want to rephrase those categories as *professional, popular, and prophetic* music.

We will look at the first of those categories in this chapter, and at the other two in the chapter following.

PROFESSIONAL MUSIC-MAKING

- ### ♦ IN THE TEMPLE

  - #### – THE PSALMS

    Most of the music described in the Old Testament was composed and performed by professional musicians, or at least by people who were musically especially gifted by God. The book of Psalms is representative of a much larger corpus of professionally written anthems, carefully composed for use in the temple. The fourteen acrostic poems in the Old Testament indicate the measure of thoughtful artistry that probably lies behind the whole collection of psalms.

    Who sang the psalms? Although they were sung by the people (compare Mt 26:30, which probably refers to *Psalms 113 to 118*), they were probably intended more for performance by the professional choristers in the temple. The psalmist describes a *"solemn procession"* into the temple, and says that *"the singers were in front, the minstrels last, and between them maidens playing timbrels"* (Ps 68:24-26).

---

[73] Dr. Bruce H. Leafblad, in an article, <u>What Sound Church Music</u>, "Christianity Today", May 19, 1978, pg. 18.

At least some of those singers and musicians were Levites; they had their own chambers in the temple and were exempt from all other temple service - in other words, they had a full-time ministry in music, and they were ranked equal in importance with the priests who fulfilled other temple functions. They were on duty day and night, so that the sound of music was never absent from the temple (1 Ch 9:33-34).

The singers were accompanied by skilled musicians who played lyres, harps, cymbals, trumpets, and other instruments (1 Ch 15:16; 25:1-8; 2 Ch 29:25-28; compare also Ezr 2:65; 3:10-11).

The scene described in the passage from Ezra (of the musicians and choristers performing when the builders laid the foundation of the temple) reflects a widespread practice in the ancient world. The myth of Amphion with his magic lyre probably grew out of this very old practice of celebrating the beginnings of a wall or a city, a house or a temple, with music. The ancients believed that sweet melody would attract the favour of heaven upon the enterprise. It was a noble concept, and for Israel at least, a valid one.

♦ PROFESSIONAL MUSICIANS

Notice again that the temple musicians and choristers were highly trained and skilled performers. The scriptures place some emphasis on this; see *1 Chronicles 25:7; Psalm 33:2-3.*

Furthermore, they were placed under directors who were responsible for maintaining the highest possible level of performance (1 Ch 15:22; 2 Ch 34:12; and compare also the many references to *"the chief musician"* in the titles of the psalms).

The goal of that disciplined achievement was not merely artistic satisfaction, but rather the glory of God. A spiritual dynamic, not merely an aesthetic one, was their quest. Their efforts were honoured by God, for the skilled performance of music in Israel became a source of

– ENHANCED SPIRITUAL POWER

See *1 Samuel 16:14-23; 2 Kings 3:15.* Notice that this is contrary to the modern popular notion that spiritual power is found only where worship is unplanned, unstructured, and amateur. Undoubtedly the presence of God can be experienced in such a free environment; but some of the greatest outpourings of spiritual power in the Bible are associated rather with the structured performances of skilled artists.

– DIVINE GLORY AND SPIRITUAL UNITY

See *2 Chronicles 5:11-14*. Notice the formal statement -

> "It was the duty of the trumpeters and singers to make themselves heard in unison in praise and thanksgiving to the Lord."

That was not a spontaneous nor unrehearsed performance. On the contrary, those Levitical musicians and choristers had spent *ten years*[74] honing their skills in preparation for the dedication of the temple (compare 1 Ch 6:31-32). They were highly skilled, dedicated artists. And the result of that disciplined and beautiful performance?

> "The house of the Lord was filled with a cloud, so that the priests could not stand to minister because of the cloud, for the glory of the Lord filled the house of God."

I am not saying, of course, that the glory of God fell upon them merely because their music and song were flawless. Rather, by offering to God the finest gift of praise they were able to present, in conjunction with fervent devotion, strong faith, and sincere prayer, they moved God to a greater manifestation of his presence and power than a careless performance would have attracted.

---

[74] See 1 Ch 23:1-5, which describes David's organising of the 4,000 choristers (970 BC); then 2 Ch 2:1 (970); to 2 Ch 3:1-2 (966); to 2 Ch 7:1-3 (960).

- **VICTORY IN BATTLE**

    See *2 Chronicles 20:21-28*. Notice that Jehoshaphat did not invite the entire army to sing. Instead, he

    > "**appointed** those who were to sing to the Lord and to praise him in holy array, as they went before the army."

    The troops may well have sung also; but the spiritual focus was upon the professional Levites, garbed in their choir robes (the insignia of their holy office of praise) and singing their well-rehearsed anthem-

    > "Give thanks to the Lord, for his steadfast love endures forever" (compare 1 Ch 16:7 and the Psalm that follows, verses 8-34).

♦ **CALLED BY GOD**

Notice that the temple musicians were gifted and chosen by God. "Calling for volunteers" to fill the ranks of the choir or the orchestra is not a biblical concept. Only those who are recognisably chosen by God should be appointed to ministry functions in the church. The operative words in scripture are "pray" and "send" - that is, don't just announce that there are vacancies in the music department, but "**Pray** that God will **send**" the people of his own choice to serve the church in music and song (Mt 9:37-38).

The natural speaking gift of a great orator will not by itself make him a great preacher. Indeed, if he is not called by God, if he is not dedicated to the glory of God, if he does not have a passion to bring Christ to the people, his eloquence will bring to the church not life but spiritual death. A stumble-tongued speaker who has been sent by God will be immeasurably more effective.

The same is true of those who seek to minister to the church in music and song. The church should not tolerate mere performers or entertainers, no matter how skilled they may be. Rather it must reach out for those who can sing and play under the favour of God because they have been appointed by him. It is likely that they will also be naturally gifted (despite the story of Balaam, God does not often send a donkey to do a man's work); but natural skills must yield the primary place to the call of God.

Bruce Leafblad says,

> "The role of music in the church is nothing more than, nothing less than, nothing other than the work of the church: ministry to the Lord; ministry to the body of Christ; and ministry to the world for which Christ died."[75]

He suggests that churches often choose their music for reasons other than genuine ministry - such false reasons as popular appeal, church tradition, spiritual entertainment, or artistic excellence. Those things may all have a place in helping the church to find the best music for each occasion, but none of them should be allowed to control the choice of music. Neither popularity, nor art, nor tradition should be the criterion, but effective ministry.

In one of his seminars at the great "*Jesus '79*" conference in Sydney, Dr. Jesse Peterson declared he had found few church choirs where the members all had a sense of being involved in a vital ministry. Mostly, people joined the choir for their own pleasure, and attended rehearsals, and even the Sunday services, at their own convenience. That is scandalous. Yet often the people are not at fault, but their leaders. No attempt has been made to define the purpose of the choir and to give it a vital ministry function in the church. Why do you have a choir? What is its real purpose? Does it fulfil any purpose? What role does God have for the choir in your church?

Until questions like those are answered the choir will remain in a spiritual limbo, and its members will always lack incentive. But if church and choir together conceive an essential ministry-function for the choir, if they get a Spirit-inspired vision of the place that music and song should have in the church, the result will be choristers who are strongly motivated to consecrate themselves to serve only God in their song.

♦ IN THE CHURCH

Apart from the Apocalypse, neither formal choirs nor a worship liturgy are mentioned in the New Testament. However, the church was patterned at least partly upon the synagogue and upon the temple, and in both of those

---

[75] Ibid.

music had a prominent function. Indeed it is surprising to survey the data and discover just how much importance was given to the "singers" *in the temple liturgy*. *I have already shown they were appointed to this ministry exclusively and were rostered on duty both day and night. Their main function was simply to praise God without ceasing (1 Ch 9:27-34).*

That pattern, according to the Apocalypse, continues in the heavenly realm, where mighty choirs of angels and trumpeters thunder their praises without ceasing around the throne of God. Indeed, even a silence of 30 minutes was so remarkable its occurrence has been recorded forever! (Re 8:1).

Mind you, not everyone agrees that such an unseemly noise is appropriate for the church -

- **MUSIC BANNED**

    The 18th century commentator Matthew Henry, for example, had this to say about Israel's sacred orchestras -

    > "There were, in compliance with the temper of that dispensation, a great variety of musical instruments used, `*harps, psalteries, cymbals*' (1 Ch 25:1,6), and here was one that `*lifted up the horn*' (vs. 5), that is, used wind-music. <u>The bringing of such concerts of music into the worship of God now is what none pretend to.</u>[76] But those who use such concerts for their own entertainment should feel themselves obliged to preserve them always free from anything that savours of immorality or profaneness, by this consideration, that time was when they were sacred; and then those were justly condemned who brought them into common use (Am 6:5), `*They invented to themselves instruments of music like David*'."

---

[76] The emphasis is mine. Elsewhere in his commentaries Matthew Henry draws a similar contrast between the musical worship-style of the temple and the non-musical style of the 18th century evangelical church.

Many of the Puritan leaders banned all kinds of music (apart from the unaccompanied voice) from their churches. Some refused to sing anything except the biblical psalms, and even then all melodic expression was forbidden, apart from a rigid chant-form. Something of that is expressed in this striking passage from John Calvin -

> "We do not here condemn speaking and singing, but rather strongly commend them, provided they are associated with the heart's affection. For thus do they exercise the mind in thinking of God and keep it attentive - unstable and variable as it is, and readily relaxed and diverted in different directions, unless it be supported by various helps ...
>
> "It is evident that the practice of singing in church ... is not only a very ancient one but also was in use among the apostles (1 Co 14:15; Cl 3:16) ... Yet Augustine testifies that this practice was not universal when he states that the church of Milan first began to sing only under Ambrose ... Then the remaining Western churches followed Milan ... He also indicates in the second book of his Retractions *that the practice was taken up in Africa in his day: `A certain Hilary,' he says, `an ex-tribune, attacked with malicious reproof, wherever he could, the custom, just then begun at Carthage, of singing hymns from the book of Psalms at the altar ...* '
>
> "But surely, if the singing be tempered to that gravity which is fitting in the sight of God and the angels, it both lends dignity and grace to sacred actions ... Yet we should be very careful that our ears be not more attentive to the melody than our minds to the spiritual meaning of the words. Augustine also admits in another place that he was so disturbed by this danger that he sometimes wished to see established the custom observed by Athanasius, who orders the reader

to use so little inflection of the voice that he would sound more like a speaker than a singer. But when he recalled how much benefit singing had brought him, he inclined to the other side.

> "Therefore, when this moderation is maintained, it is without doubt a most holy and salutary practice. On the other hand, such songs as have been composed only for sweetness and delight of the ear are unbecoming to the majesty of the church and cannot but displease God to the highest degree."[77]

It is not difficult to imagine what those old Reformers and Puritans would think about the worship practices of many modern charismatic meetings! Their sentiments are zealously endorsed by various groups of Christians who still banish all instrumental music from their churches. The dogmas of these modern lovers of the unaided voice are akin to those of C. H. Spurgeon-

> "David appears to have had a peculiarly tender remembrance of the `*the singing*' of the pilgrims, and assuredly it is the most delightful part of worship and that which comes nearest to the adoration of heaven. What a degradation to supplant the intelligent song of the whole congregation by the theatrical prettiness of a quartette, the refined niceties of a choir, or the blowing off of wind from inanimate balloons and pipes! We might as well pray by machinery as praise by it."[78]

---

[77] From Calvin's 16th century Institutes of the Christian Religion (III.20); ed. by J. T. McNeill; tr. by Ford Battles; Westminster Press, Philadelphia. The selection above was taken from The Christian Life: John Calvin, ed. By J. H. Leith; Harper & Row, New York; 1984; pg. 71-73.

[78] From his commentary on Psalm 42:4

Happily, not all past leaders were so stern -

1.2.2 MUSIC ENCOURAGED

Martin Luther was not impressed by those who wanted to remove music-making from the church. He had some caustic things to say about them -

> "I am not satisfied with him who despises music, as all fanatics do; for music is an endowment and gift of God, not a gift of men ... I am not of the opinion that all the arts are to be overthrown and cast aside by the gospel, as some super-spiritual people protest."[79]

Many times in his writings Luther placed the study and use of music almost on a level with theology. He would not consider ordaining a young man into the ministry until he had first studied and practised music. Luther reckoned that the example set in Israel's temple was fully transferable to the church, and that Christians should make abundant use of choirs and instruments of all sorts -

> "Of old the use of music was sacred and was adapted to divine matters ... For by it also the evil spirit of Saul was driven off (1 Sa 16:23), and the prophetic spirit was given to Elisha (2 Kg 3:15) ... (They) praised God with singing and playing, with poetry and all kinds of string music ... Christian musicians should let their singing and playing to the praise of the Father of all grace sound forth with joy from their organs and whatever other beloved musical instruments there are (recently invented and given by God), of which neither David nor Solomon, neither Persia, Greece, nor Rome, knew anything. Amen!"[80]

---

[79] What Luther Says; #3091, 3095.

[80] Ibid. #3094, 3095, 3100. In the same place there are a dozen other selections, all showing Luther's high regard for the spiritual power godly music can exert upon performers, participants, and hearers alike.

The example of Israel, the example of the angelic choirs, the example of history, surely show there is nothing displeasing to God in the sound of joyful music in the church. The Fathers certainly had no scruples on the matter, and from the first century on there are references to liturgical music and to sacred songs.[81]

Putting this all together, it could be concluded

- that there is a place for professional musicians and singers in the church;
- that for some this will be a full-time ministry, while for others only part-time;
- that all church musicians should be dedicated to the glory of God;
- that they should all be called by God to serve him through music;
- that disciplined rehearsal and artistic excellence are part of that call; and
- that they should all strive not merely to perform well but to fulfil a ministry through their music.

Professional music ministry within the church can be defined then as having five aspects:

- to minister to the Lord, in worship, praise, thanksgiving, and adoration.
- to minister to the church, in exhortation, encouragement, inspiration, and instruction.
- to minister to the unsaved, in witness, proclamation, warning, and love.

---

[81] See the addendum. Also Eusebius writes (c. 300), " ... how many psalms and hymns, written by the faithful brethren from the beginning, celebrate Christ the Word of God, speaking of him as Divine" (5:28). Notice the words "from the beginning", and the reference to "hymns" as well as "psalms".

- to provide an example to the congregation in worship, commitment, enthusiasm, and maturity.
- to help the church to create a musical expression that is uniquely its own.

By this, I do not mean that the church should forsake contemporary or secular musical forms; but that the church, no matter what use it makes of secular inventions, should develop a style and quality of music that is at once recognisably its own. Not recognisable because it sounds "religious" *or* "*churchy*", *but because it has beauty, joy, depth, and life, that "worldly" music simply cannot emulate.*

What is true of the church generally should be true also of each local church. The music in your church should be in some respects unlike that in any other. Resist the temptation to copy other successful churches, to do what they do, to sound the way they sound. Have the courage to identify the peculiar combination of musical talents God has brought into your congregation and, with God's help, to blend them into a beautiful melody unlike that heard anywhere else. The God of a million different snowflakes has many brilliant ideas to share with you about the music in your church, if you will take the time to listen to him.[82]

---

[82] I do not mean, of course, that everything should be new. There is a place also for the old and the familiar, and to utilise the discoveries and creations of others. The wise worship leader, like a well-instructed scribe, will know how to "bring out of his treasure both what is new and what is old" (Mt 13:52).

Chapter Nine

THE SOUND OF PROPHECY

We turn now to the two other kinds of musical expression mentioned by Paul; those that I have paraphrased as *popular* and *prophetic*.

POPULAR MUSIC-MAKING

♦ ABOUNDING JOY

Outside the temple (with its professional musicians, dancers, and singers) there was a nation full of people who honoured God with their own spontaneous music-making. The Old Testament contains many descriptions of scenes like the following -

> *"All Israel were making merry before God with all their might, with songs and lyres and harps and tambourines and cymbals and trumpets" (1 Ch 13:8); and this,*

> *"So all Israel brought up the ark of the covenant of the Lord with shouting, to the sound of the horns, trumpets, and cymbals, and made loud music on harps and lyres" (15:28).*

The Israelites were able to sustain such popular singing and dancing before the Lord for several days -

> *"The people ... kept the feast (for) seven days with great gladness; and the Levites and the priests praised the Lord day by day, singing with all their might to the Lord ... Then the whole assembly agreed together to keep the feast for another seven days; so they kept it for another seven days with gladness ... and the whole assembly ... rejoiced" (2 Ch 30:21-25).*

God was as much pleased by that kind of unstructured worship as he was by the formal and skilled liturgies of the temple. When the people were united and sincere in spontaneous praise, when their folk songs and dances were offered as a sacrifice of joy to God, they could attract his glory as well as could the finest temple anthem (compare Ps 133:1-3).

♦ AMONG CHRISTIANS

There are several examples in the New Testament of hymns that were apparently written for and sung by the people: Luke 1:46-55, 68-79; 2:14, 29-32; 1 Timothy 1:17; 6:15-16; Philippians 2:5-11; Ephesians 1:3-14; Romans 8:31-39; 1 Corinthians 13:4-7.

Not all scholars would accept all those passages as examples of early hymns, and some scholars would suggest other passages; none the less, there is agreement that such hymns are embedded in the New Testament, and show that from its very beginning the church was a place of community song.

Since then, music-making by the people has been part of the experience of every generation of Christians, especially during times of spiritual renewal. Indeed, those times have often produced a new musical expression in the church, such as the hymn-singing that came out of the Reformation in the 16th and 17th centuries, and out of the Wesleyan revivals of the 18th century. Then the evangelism of the 19th century produced the *"gospel song"*; while the pentecostal/charismatic revival of our time has sparkled with *"choruses"* and *"scripture songs"*. Thus we now have access to a marvellous heritage of popular Christian music - that is, of music written not for performance by professional musicians but for the people to sing joyously together.

Both kinds of music-making, the professional and the popular, are given to the church by God. It is a mistake to insist, as some do, that the glory of God rests only upon the latest songs and choruses, and only upon unrehearsed congregational music-making. It is equally mistaken to suppose that God is glorified only by serious and exalted music that is professionally performed.

A wise church will not permit its congregation to become mere spectators of a worship performance by the pastors and musicians; but neither will it allow worship to become more revelry than reverence, more sound than substance.

♦ OLD AND NEW

It is sensible neither to cling wholly to the past nor to the present. It is also sensible to realise that the church cannot help but reflect the musical styles of the surrounding secular culture, even though in its adoption of current musical forms it modifies them for its own use.

Thus Dale McGlellan writes:

> "Scripture, and not culture, should be our authority - about that there is no argument. But scripture says very little about how worship should be conducted, and it seems unavoidable that culture would provide sources for musical style as well as many other things in a service. This idea that there is a dichotomy between cultural influences and spiritual worship would assume that the primitive church was uninfluenced in their choice of music by their cultural milieu.
>
> "Although we cannot be certain how the early church sang, since recordings from that era are scarce, it is not likely that they began immediately to compose brand new music wholly unlike what they had sung in the synagogue prior to the day of Pentecost.
>
> "The guitar and chorus syndrome of the present time is so completely reflective of the modern culture, which has produced more than its share of three-chord millionaires, that I am astounded that anyone can consider this form to have been raised up by the Holy Spirit or that it (alone) is a 'Christ-centred' style."[83]

Admittedly, the locale of a church, the cultural experience of the people who comprise its membership, the limits of the skills of its musicians, will all shape what is musically possible for that church. So it may be that some congregations will never hear the sound of Bach while others will never hear the sound of pop. Yet they will all be poorer for that loss.

> "There is no good or bad music stylistically. There are, of course, bad lyrics and bad musical lines, as well as good lyrics and good musical lines. I really don't

---

[83] From an article in Agora magazine, Volume Two, Number Three, pg. 17. The publisher and date are unknown to me.

consider country music better than rock or rock worse than gospel. The task of the musicians is to discover where their audiences are, and to minister to them at that level."[84]

It would be good for congregations that are not familiar with the glorious traditional and classical music of the church to be slowly introduced to it and educated to appreciate it. It would be equally good for congregations who sit in church as silent spectators to become roused in joy and involved in worship, by learning how to use the sometimes exciting and powerful music that has come out of the charismatic renewal in our time.

The best experience surely arises out of a dynamic blend of the old with the new, the professional with the popular, so that every person becomes deeply involved in glorifying God through their music-making.

Yet the sound of music in the church will still be spiritually disappointing unless it also has a third quality -

PROPHETIC MUSIC-MAKING

Paul describes what should happen when

> "the whole church assembles ... and an unbeliever or an outsider enters."

Before the meeting has ended, the visitor should be:

> *"convicted by all, called to account by all, and the secrets of his heart should be disclosed, so that falling on his face he will worship God and cry out that God is really among you." (1 Co 14:23-25)*

That admirable result was probably as infrequent in ancient times as it is in ours. And the reason is the same: a lack of prophetic quality. The condition, says Paul, that leads to irresistible conversion of the outsider is that "everyone prophesies"; *that is, a prophetic mantle should rest upon the worshipping community, the sound of prophecy should be heard in every*

---

[84] Jesse Peterson.

word they speak, whether reading scripture, praying, teaching, giving revelation, or making music (verse 26).

Music should be prophecy!

That is a surprising concept to many people, yet it is well-supported in scripture, which describes three kinds of prophetic musical expression—

- ♦ **BY MUSIC ALONE**

    that is, without words, like David's musicians:

    "Musicians were set apart for the service who could <u>prophesy</u> with lyres, harps, and cymbals ... under the direction of Asaph, who <u>prophesied</u> under the command of the king ... they <u>prophesied</u> with the lyre, offering thanksgiving and praise to the Lord" (1 Ch 25:1,3).

Oh! that all of our musicians would identify themselves as prophets in the church, and would strive so to play that every melody is filled with the Holy Spirit. Then it would happen to us as it did to Elisha -

> *"When the minstrel played, the power of the Lord fell upon him." (2 Kg 3:15)*

Musicians in the church should not be treated as unimportant adjuncts to the functions of the choir, the Sunday School, and the like. They are called by God to do much more than perform, or even to perform well; they are called to prophesy through their music.

- ♦ **BY WORDS AND MUSIC**

Every song sung in the church should carry a revelation from God, both in the meaning of the words and in the way they are sung. It has often been remarked that Luther's hymns did even more than his sermons to popularise the Reformation among the peasants, artisans, and merchants of Europe.

The Israelites sang prophetic songs - that is, they sang the inspired psalms that are now part of our Bibles. We should certainly sing those same psalms in church. But we do not have to be restricted to them. The Holy Spirit has inspired the words of a multitude of songs across the ages, and he is still doing so today. Search out those songs, then make sure they are sung in a way that enables the Spirit to make powerful use of their message.

♦ BY GLOSSOLALIA

that is, singing "with the spirit", or in "other tongues".

See 1 Corinthians 14:15, and the references *to "spiritual songs"* in *Ephesians 5:19* and *Colossians 3:16*. The phenomenon of entire congregations singing together in other tongues is now widespread in the charismatic/pentecostal movement. Many feel that such *"singing in the spirit"* should be spontaneous, unstructured, unplanned, uncoordinated - that it should be the result of an invasion from heaven irresistibly carrying the people along. But scripture shows otherwise.

– FROM THE HUMAN SPIRIT

Notice that *"spirit"* in *1 Corinthians 14:15* has a small 's'. It is not the Holy Spirit but the human spirit that sings in other tongues; in other words, this is not so much a divine activity as one that is human. The song arises from within the spirits of the people, it does not fall upon them from heaven. Once a person has been baptised in the Holy Spirit and has spoken in other tongues, it becomes just as natural for his spirit to express itself in glossolalia as it is for his mind to express itself in a vernacular tongue.

That is why Paul is able to say,

"What am I to do? I will pray with the spirit *(in glossolalia)* and I will pray with the mind also *(in the vernacular)*; I will sing with the spirit, and I will sing with the mind also."

– UNDER CONTROL

Notice that whether or not he sings or speaks in tongues is entirely under his own volition. He must himself decide what to do. *"I will,"* he says, *"at different times both sing and speak in my own language or in other tongues."* The choice and the responsibility were his alone.

So whether or not a glossolalist actually exercises the gift is a matter for that person to decide. The use of glossolalia is not governed by the Holy Spirit, but by the human will. It does not depend upon an action of God; it is not determined by the choice of God, nor by some divine control over the speaker; it is fully subject to the glossolalist's personal control.

It is clear that glossolalic song occurs because the people have chosen at that moment to sing in the spirit instead of with understanding. For that reason, the length of time they sing, and the manner, are also at their discretion. They can start or stop at will; they can sing softly or loudly, sorrowfully or cheerfully; discordantly or harmoniously. All of this arises out of the people themselves; it is a voluntary not an involuntary action; it is an expression of their conscious desire to worship God *"in the spirit"*; it is not something that falls upon them unaware.

– PROMPTED BY THE HOLY SPIRIT

Now I hasten to allow that the Holy Spirit may prompt the Spirit-filled church to praise God in other tongues; he may lead the people to burst forth in glossolalic song. Indeed, it is fervently hoped that our worship will always be guided by the Spirit, that we will always be sensitive to his direction. But Paul remains adamant: *"the spirits of the prophets are subject to the prophets."* (1 Co 14:32; see also verses 26, 33 & 40).

The maintenance of order, beauty, dignity, and harmony in the church are not the responsibility of the Holy Spirit, but ours. No matter how strongly the Holy Spirit may be moving in the church, Paul's instructions make it clear that singing in tongues remains just as firmly within our control as does singing in English. The Holy Spirit never robs the church of its freeborn prerogative to select which form of song to employ in worship, and we always have liberty to determine the time, manner, and place of our song. Scripture does not permit us to abrogate that right; but it does place us under an injunction so to speak and sing under the influence of the Spirit that the church is always edified, and Christ always glorified.

– MELODIC FORM

So then, while we trust the Holy Spirit to guide us in worship, and we expect to yield him complete obedience, that worship always remains voluntary and we must accept full responsibility for our actions.

All of that is simply a background against which to say that singing in the spirit should have form. It is no more unspiritual to require that the people harmonise with each other in glossolalic song than to do so for vernacular song. It does not restrain the Holy Spirit to impose a chordal structure on glossolalic song. Worship leaders should not abandon their office just because the people are singing in tongues. They should not hesitate to give direction, to keep sweetness and grace in the worship, to restrain those who become too boisterous, to exhort those who are too lax. It is proper for worship leaders to modulate glossolalic song, to lead the people into different harmonies and melodies, to ask those who cannot conform, or whose voices are discordant, to sing softly and not to disrupt those around them.

Paul is clear that glossolalic singing is not an arbitrary miracle wrought unexpectedly by the Holy Spirit. Rather, it is beautiful praise that the Spirit-filled church itself lifts up to the glory of God. Being filled with the Holy Spirit, and having now an ability to pray or sing in other tongues, the church should seize that ability and *"strive to excel"* as it offers back to God a sacrifice of glossolalic praise (1 Co 14:12; He 13:15).

– **SPIRITUAL EXCELLENCE**

Achieving that goal of excellence will require:

> that the people be truly filled with the Holy Spirit;
>
> that the worship leader gives wise and sensitive direction, neither intruding too much nor abandoning his or her role;
>
> that the people maintain a balance, concentrating their adoration upon God while remaining aware of each other and blending with each other in song.

It is no doubt wonderful in private *"to get lost in the glory"* and to worship God in any way you please; but such liberty is not appropriate in a public service. When other people are joining with you, that is not the time (as a familiar chorus unfortunately says) to *"just forget about yourself and concentrate on him, and worship him."* Rather, hearts, hands, and voices should be raised in unison to bless the Almighty with conscious harmony and beauty.

– HEAVENLY SONG

Now a final comment about *"singing in the spirit"*. This sweet song, so lilting, so lovely, may be an answer from God to the primitive cry of the human heart for a melody truly infused with divine grace. The ancient Greeks captured that yearning in their myths about Aeolus (the god of the wind) and the magical instrument that was named after him, the Aeolian harp. Those early people sensed an awesome mystery in the strange humming harmonies of the wind-swept chords. The soft melodies seemed to promise an anthem inspired by the gods, transcending any sound that human fingers could entice from the taut strings. But of course their hopes were futile. It was after all only the sound of wind flowing over a cluster of stretched catgut in a wooden box. But we are dealing with the true heavenly wind, the eternal Spirit of God (Ac 2:2), and he is plucking the strings of our hearts. In the divine melodies he produces there is a haunting beauty, a sound of limitless freedom, a miracle of love, a splendid glory of inspired worship.[85]

---

[85] Glossolalic prayer and worship was probably known also to the ancient Israelites. There are suggestions of glossolalia in the following references: Nu 11:24-25; 1 Sa 10:5-13; 19:18-24; 2 Sa 6:13-17; 1 Kg 18:28-29; 20:35-37. The popular suspicion that the prophets were "madmen" may also suggest that they used glossolalia (Je 29:26; Ho 9:7; and cp. also Is 8:19).

Addendum

A THING OF BEAUTY

INTRODUCTION

Unhappy in love, with much of his major work scorned by the critics, racked with consumption, John Keats died in Rome in 1821, aged only 26, and attended by only one friend. But despite the tragedy of his young life, Keats left behind him a legacy of poems almost unequalled, and certainly unsurpassed, in the English language.

From one of his poems, which was savagely criticised when it was first published, has come a line that is perhaps as familiar as any other ever written. It begins his poem *Endymion* -

> A thing of beauty is a joy for ever:
>
> Its loveliness increases; it will never
>
> Pass into nothingness; but still will keep
>
> A bower quiet for us, and a sleep
>
> Full of sweet dreams, and health, and quiet breathing.

Who would deny the joy of beauty? But is it the highest pleasure? There are three kinds of joy possible in this world -

- ### THE JOY OF THE PHYSICAL

Satisfaction of our physical needs is necessarily our first and most urgent quest. But no one can find happiness by focussing on the flesh alone. In the end the sweetest physical pleasure fails to satisfy. Why is that so? Because of two problems -

  - #### SATIATION

    The more physical pleasure is pursued, the less it satisfies. Those who gorge themselves at a meal quickly discover that where they hoped to find pleasure they have reaped instead pain! They are like the three things that are never content, and the four that never cry, *"Enough!"* or like the two *daughters of the leech* which never stop saying, *"Give! Give!"* (Pr 30:15). They are like *"dogs with a ravenous appetite that are never filled"* (Is 56:11,12); they stand among those who *"when they have finished drinking must then rush into a sexual orgy"* (Ho 4:18). Such are all who think that lasting fulfilment can be found by making the belly their god (cp. Ph 3:18-19).

– **ABSURDITY**

All physical appetites mock our pretensions to dignity and nobility; indeed, the more necessary or powerful the pleasure, the more absurd it seems. Consider for example:

> <u>*eating*</u>: we don't like to watch people actually eating - it is considered very bad manners to do so - and we disguise the act as much as we can with countless rules of etiquette; then there is

> <u>*coition*</u>: about which the saintly Sir Thomas Browne (1605-1682) said:

> "I could be content that we might procreate like trees, without conjunction, or that there were any way to perpetuate the world without this trivial and vulgar way of coition: it is the foolishest act a wise man commits in all his life; nor is there anything that will more deject his cooled imagination, when he shall consider what an odd and unworthy piece of folly he hath committed."[86]

None of us are about to abandon such physical pleasures as are available to us; yet, because of their manifest shortcomings, sensitive people find themselves driven to search for a higher happiness in

---

[86] Religio Medici Pt. 2:9.

- ♦ **THE JOY OF THE BEAUTIFUL**
  - **A THING OF BEAUTY**

    The capacity to create and recognise *"a thing of beauty"* is one of the major things that separates us from the brute beasts. We know the difference between the lovely and the ugly, and we respond to them with joy or disgust. This is unique to human beings; it is a quality of perception possessed by no other creature. On Earth, only men and women can create and recognise art.

    Among all the arts music is reckoned the highest; thus the English dramatist and poet, William Congreve (1670-1728), said -

    > "Music hath charms to soothe a savage breast
    >
    > To soften rocks, or bend a knotted oak."

  - and the English philosopher and journalist, Herbert Spencer (1820-1903), wrote-

    > "Music must take rank as the highest of the fine arts - as the one which, more than any other, ministers to human welfare."

    Now this ability to rejoice in beauty at once confronts us with

  - **A THING OF MYSTERY**

    There is a mystery in the gladness beauty brings that goes beyond the merely natural. Thus Sir Thomas Browne reckoned he could hear the voice of God in all kinds of music -

    > "For even that vulgar and tavern music, which makes one man merry, another mad, strikes in me a deep fit of devotion, and a profound contemplation of the first Composer, for there is something in it of divinity more than the ear discovers."[87]

---

[87] Ibid.

Yet all who reach out for loveliness in life find another truth: beauty is also

– A THING OF DISAPPOINTMENT

Even the joy of music must fail of full satisfaction, for to the grieving it may bring only more sorrow, or to the tone deaf it is a mockery. Thus the great 18th century raconteur and lexicographer Samuel Johnson, who had no feeling for music, heard a lady play exquisitely on a harpsichord. When she asked him if he were fond of music, he replied -

> "No, madam; but of all the noises I think music is the least disagreeable."

But even the most renowned connoisseur of music will one day go the way of all flesh. Then, when death deprives us of our senses, the joy of music must fail for every person:

> "Remember your Creator while you are still young, <u>before</u> aches and pains beset you, <u>before</u> you get old and start saying of the years, `I have no pleasure in them.'

then he goes on to describe those years:

> "Sunlight and moonlight and starlight become dim ... the guards at the gate of the house tremble, and the strong men are bowed over, and the women who grind the flour stop working because they are few, and those who peer through the windows see dimly. The doors to the street are shut, the noise of grinding is scarcely heard, the twittering of birds fades away, and <u>the sound of music is known no more</u>." (Ec 12:1-4)

Thus all earthly joys save one must vanish, and that one is

♦ THE JOY OF THE SPIRITUAL

This joy is what John Milton called "the beatific vision", and it is the best of all, for all; it never satiates, it never wearies. King David understood this joy -

> *"One thing I ask of the Lord, and this will I seek after: that I might live in the house of the Lord all the days of my life, and always gaze upon the beauty of the Lord!"*

If "a thing of beauty is a joy for ever", what could surpass the joy of gaining an open vision of the God of glory! But that vision can never be known while the soul is still imprisoned by guilt, death, and judgment. Thus we must turn to Jesus, who alone is the Restorer of eternal beauty. To believe in him, as Peter said, is indeed inexpressible joy!

CONCLUSION

In March 1631, while ill from the sickness that a few days later would take his life, John Donne wrote a poem entitled A Hymn to God my God" -

"Since I am coming to that holy room

Where, with the choirs of saints for evermore,

I shall be made thy music; as I come

I tune my instrument here at the door,

And what I must do then, think now before."

What song will you sing beyond the grave? A lamentation? Or a hymn of joy? John Donne, like all good musicians, knew that the time to tune your instrument is not when you are called upon to face the judges, but before.

We should now, not then, allow Jesus to fill our hearts with the melodies of heaven, sung sweetly in tune, by those for whom such song has become their most natural sound, to the glory of God for ever.

Chapter Ten

PRINCIPLES OF WORSHIP

***Texts*:** John 4:23; Romans 12:1; 1 Corinthians 14:24-26 - note that this is the only description we have of a New Testament church worship service.

The first thing to notice is an idea raised in the previous chapter: ***spontaneous growth results from true worship***. Paul's description of visitors coming into the Corinthian church and almost at once falling upon their faces under conviction of sin is perhaps hyperbolic, but it nonetheless shows the potential that lies in true Spirit-filled worship. Certain principles can be seen ...

- **TRUE WORSHIP HAS A PROPHETIC QUALITY**

As I have said before, the secret at Corinth seems to have been this: ***there was a mantle of prophecy resting on every part of the service.*** Where that prophetic quality is missing, the worship service must be deemed in some respect to have failed. It shows that pentecostal worship should be supernatural worship, creating an undeniable sense of the presence of God. If sincere people who come among us cannot sense the divine presence, then our worship must be deemed unsuccessful.

- **TRUE WORSHIP HAS A LIFE-GIVING QUALITY**

There is a release of life in the assembly of the saints which is absent from individual Christians. By the universal law of God, which is equally applicable in the natural and spiritual realms, that life has power to beget life. Indeed, real life always produces new life. Hence Paul inevitably pictures the worshipping church as a growing church! At once we learn two things -

> *The local church is pre-eminently a place of worship, not evangelism, except that it will do its best evangelism through worship. It is useful to remember that the "gospel service" of modern times (with its "altar call") is a recent innovation. Prior*

to the 19th century such practices were virtually unknown in the church - yet it continued to expand world-wide! Never forget how the early church, lacking nearly all our modern conveniences, and in an age of persecution, still flourished. Though often forbidden to evangelise, prevented from holding public services, obliged to meet in caves, dens, cellars, attics, and graveyards, yet the church grew through the sheer power of its worship.

Therefore, though a church may lack many things, it can still grow through good worship. By contrast, see the devastating effect of bad worship! (1 Co 14:23). Now outsiders and unbelievers, instead of being attracted to the church and eagerly joining the worshipping throng, walk away in disgust, reckoning the company of Christians to be lunatics! Which response does the worship in your church elicit?

♦ TRUE WORSHIP IS RATIONAL AND IRRATIONAL

See *1 Corinthians 14:13-15*, where Paul highlights two essential components of pentecostal worship: the *irrational* and the *rational*.

We must spurn this world's idolatrous worship of human reason. The church has been too heavily influenced by the idea that human reason is the best gift of God; yet there is an irrational dimension[88] in God himself, aspects of his being and nature that defy all human explanation. Think, for example, about the following:

- there is his self-generation, that is, the idea that God is the sole cause of his own existence;

- or consider his eternity, that God has always been, is, and always will be;

---

[88] That is, a dimension that transcends the boundaries of the human mind, which cannot be encompassed within the confines of human reason.

- or what about his infinity, that God has no boundaries, no beginning, no end, expanding without horizon through space, and throughout time?
- most baffling of all is his foreknowledge, for how can even God know what has not yet been?
- then there is his sovereignty, that despite the chaos of the nations, and the disruptions in heaven, yet the Almighty bends everything toward his will, and not the slightest part of his purpose can ever be thwarted!

There are other mysteries in God, which pummel the brain into fragments whenever one tries to grasp them mentally. I can easily accept their truth, but my mind falls apart when I try to comprehend them, they defy reason, they mock understanding, they baffle logic.

Yet that ought not to surprise us, because even at our own level the best things in life are irrational (cp. Pr 30:18-19). Can the loveliness of a rose be measured by a mathematical theorem; can human immortality ever be demonstrated in a laboratory; can a physicist's formula ever compose a glorious symphony; can the magic of romance be pulled out of a test tube; has any philosopher ever been able to explain a mother's joy in her baby's laugh? All these are the sweetest things in life, yet they defy reason, they scorn logical analysis!

I do not mean that we should despise reason, nor cast aside everything that reflects rational behaviour. That would be true nonsense. Because it is (I hope) a piece of intelligent writing, must I throw my book into the rubbish bin? Hardly! There is plenty of room in Christian worship for many things that depend upon good sense and sound reasoning. But woe to worship when nothing else can be found there! How spiritually barren, how desolate and bleak, how much like a desert, will that church become!

Threaded through all genuine worship there must be some elements of the irrational, and to this end the Holy Spirit has placed in the church the gift of tongues. The presence of irrational glossolalia in worship keeps us in touch with the supernatural and with the infinite. It stops the church from prostrating itself before the altar of human reason. It teases our pretensions to wisdom. It forces us to acknowledge that we are yet little better than children looking through a piece of smoky glass (1 Co 13:9-12). It forces us to keep on exalting most highly the wondrously irrational qualities of *faith, hope, and love* (vs. 13).

When glossolalia fails, worship tends to become ever more structured and controlled, ever more stilted and conformist, ever less spontaneous and joyful.

- ### ♦ TRUE WORSHIP HAS FORM AND FREEDOM

    See *1 Corinthians 12:28*, and notice the mixture of

    – the <u>mundane</u>: apostles; teachers; helpers; administrators.

        You could walk into many churches, look around, and describe them in those four terms. And having said that much about them, there is nothing more to say; those four terms embrace their total identity. That is, nothing ever happens that lies beyond the ability of a human mind and a skilled hand. No work is done, no voice is heard, that could only have come from God. Everything lies within the boundaries of human wisdom and human achievement. To put it bluntly, a group of atheists could copy everything some churches do, and an observer would not see any difference.

        But the end result of such naturalism is an arid intellectualism, a sterile formalism.

    – the <u>miraculous</u>: prophets; healers; miracles; glossolalists.

        You could walk into some pentecostal churches, look around, and then describe them entirely in those four terms. But if nothing more than those four things can be said about a church, then the result will be a crass and shallow emotionalism, which may lead on to ignorant fanaticism. The church therefore must be zealous for two things:

        <u>good order</u> (see 1 Co 14:6,26,33,40).

        Do not make the mistake of equating the "irrational" with the "unreasonable", nor with the ugly and the disorderly. True worship will display dignity, grace, beauty, a pleasing shape, and a balanced structure. In the end, lasting spiritual power depends upon this (vs. 12). Note how God wanted the priests of Israel to be clothed with *"glory and splendour"* (Ex 28:2,40), and he gave that nation a worship-style filled with zest, but set within a framework of majesty. It is an example that the church should copy.

divine intervention

Full space must be left for the Holy Spirit, like the wind, to *"blow wherever he pleases!"* Thus intelligent planning and charismatic spontaneity must be held in balance together. The one must not be allowed to swamp the other; worship should be like neither a perfectly manicured park, nor an unweeded jungle, but rather a pleasing amalgam of form and freedom, a fine blending of the human and the divine.

♦ TRUE WORSHIP WILL BE PARTICIPATORY

There must be leadership and authority, but we dare not allow the people to become merely passive components of a liturgy. True worship will actively involve the entire congregation (vs. 26). Scripture leaves no room either for

a performance by professional clergy, with the congregation behaving like mere spectators; or for

an irresponsible individualism, which scorns the authority of those to whom God has given leadership in the church and disturbs the "symphony" of worship.

Nonetheless, place must be allowed for any individual, great or small, to speak as the oracle of God to the church (vs. 26,30). The meaning of the latter verse is in some ways a mystery. Perhaps even the Corinthians were puzzled by the disturbing injunction *"let the first be silent"*! Presumably Paul did *not* mean that we could interrupt each other whenever we please! But how he actually intended his instruction to be put into practise remains unknown.

But one principle is quite clearly established: the Lord is not obliged to speak only through "official" channels; he may choose to express his will through any member of the congregation.

There is no doubt some peril in that kind of openness; but the tension created here is no more than exists in other places in scripture (for example, in the argument between divine sovereignty and human freedom). How should we handle this tension? Some churches become so ordered that they remove all the friction biblical principles usually cause; they become so structured that nothing remains but chill spiritual death. Others become so free that anyone can speak with an equal voice, and they reap an inescapable harvest of confusion (cp. vs. 33). The proper course is to maintain a balance between authority and liberty; that is, to acknowledge that God usually works through proper channels, yet always to leave space for the Holy Spirit to speak or act through the humblest member of the congregation.

♦ TRUE WORSHIP IS NOT IMPULSIVE

There is a strange idea floating around that true pentecostal worship requires the surrender of personal volition, that it should result mostly (if not entirely) from momentary inspiration. But should we just yield to impulse, whenever we feel that we are being "moved" by the Spirit? Paul certainly did not think so; see *1 Corinthians 12:1-3*, and notice how he insists that hallmark of paganism is stamped upon yielding to mindless urges, doing whatever one feels "moved" to do. Yet some charismatics crave to be "taken over" by the Spirit, as if that represents the quintessence of piety!

Paul says rather that the *best* sign that you are truly Spirit-filled is not a *loss* of self-control, but rather the *gaining* of it! (Ga 5:22-23).

We should do *nothing* just because we feel "moved"; instead, we should back off and take time to "prove" whether or not God is speaking (cp. 1 Th 5:20-21).

Those who are wise learn how to worship God with their whole self: body, mind, and spirit.

♦ TRUE WORSHIP WILL BE EUCHARISTIC

Let us at once draw a distinction between mere emotional arousal and true joy in the Holy Spirit. Some worship leaders so stir up the emotions that they leave the people drained of energy. How can you tell the difference? As we saw in *Chapter Seven* above

> the one glorifies man, the other God; the one exhausts, the other edifies; the one depends upon a tightly controlled and manipulated programme, the other upon a free flow of worship.

Godly joy in worship will leave people refreshed and alive. Emotion in worship should not be aroused to *produce* the Spirit, but rather should be the *product* of the Spirit, in the spiritual fruit of *"love, joy, and peace."* The mark of a genuine worship leader will be an easy grace rather than a frenetic compulsion, aggressive, demanding.

See *1 Corinthians 14:17*, where the verb is *"eucharisteo"* (to give thanks). Paul implies that unless worship has this "eucharistic" quality, it hardly deserves the name. That idea leads us to a wonderful discovery. What is the chief image of God in us? Our voices, especially when they are aroused in praise to God! For example, consider the strange use of *kabod* in *Psalm 16:9; 30:12; 57:8; 108:1,3; 149:5,6*; where the idea seems to be that the chief glory of man is the sound of his voice raised in praise to God. There seems also to be a suggestion in this use of *kabod* of *glossolalic* praise. We are never clothed with so much dignity as when we are standing in the presence of God, hands upraised, praising him aloud with all our heart, and especially in the heavenly language of the Spirit!

♦ TRUE WORSHIP IS FULL OF MELODY

Despite the opinion of some churches, which frown on or forbid the use of musical instruments, the sound of music is pleasing to God. Is not the entire universe filled with unending music? (Jb 38:7; and notice how unusual it was for heaven to be silent, Re 8:1!)

Likewise, from the beginning the Lord desired his house to be a place of melody and endless song. Surely it is absurd to strip the church of that joyful sound? Must every skill but that of a musician be usable in the church? Must the music-maker alone be obliged to exercise his skill only for a secular purpose and never in the house of God? If the *Psalms* are allowed to speak on the matter (e.g. Ps 150:3-5), then clearly the Lord takes joy in all manner of musical praise.

♦ TRUE WORSHIP REVEALS CHRIST

The local church is the primary expression of the "body" of Christ on earth; that is, the local church should be all that Jesus would be if he were here in person. There is no better way to accomplish this goal than so to worship God that the Saviour himself is pleased to stand among us and join in our anthems (He 2:12).

And now let me finish, as I promised in *A Cure For Snake Bite!*, with the last stanza of Sir Thomas Wyatt's song -

Now *cease* my lute: this is the last

Labour that thou and I shall waste,

And ended is that we begun.

Now is this song both sung and past:
My lute be still, for I have done.

Addendum One

THE CHURCH FATHERS

Here is a selection of quotations from the church Fathers. They show the use of Sunday as a day of worship, how the early Christians celebrated the eucharist, and other practices both good and bad. They also show that there are no new worship foibles. Just as in our day, so in the first two or three centuries, worship was sometimes shameful, sometimes sublime.

The selection is restricted to the Ante-Nicene Fathers, with a couple of closing exceptions. It is presented for your interest. I do not necessarily condone nor condemn the opinions expressed by the Fathers.

– THE EPISTLE OF BARNABUS (c. 100 A.D.)

"(God said to Israel), 'Your new moons and your sabbaths I cannot endure'... Wherefore also, we keep the eighth day with joyfulness, the day also on which Jesus rose again from the dead" (Ch. 15).

– CLEMENT OF ROME (c. 100)

" ... it behoves us to do all things in their proper order, which the Lord has commanded us to perform at stated times. He has enjoined offerings to be presented and to be performed to him, and that not thoughtlessly or irregularly, but at the appointed times and hours. Where and by whom he desires these things to be done, he himself has fixed by his own supreme will, in order that all things being piously done according to his good pleasure, may be acceptable unto him ... The layman is bound by the laws that pertain to laymen" *(First letter to the Corinthians,* Ch. 40).

– IGNATIUS (C. 100)

"Take heed then often to come together to give thanks to God, and to show forth his praise. For

when you come frequently together in the same place, the powers of Satan are destroyed, and his fiery darts urging to sin fall back ineffectual" (Letter to the Ephesians, Ch. 13) ...

"See that you follow your bishop, even as Christ Jesus does the Father, and the presbytery as you would the apostles. Reverence also your deacons, as those who are fulfilling their office by the appointment of God. Let no man do anything connected with the church without the bishop. Let only that be accepted as a proper eucharist which is administered either by the bishop, or by one to whom he has entrusted it ... It is not lawful without the bishop either to baptise, or to bring an offering, or to present a sacrifice, or to celebrate a love-feast" *(Letter to the Smyrneans, Ch.8).*

- **THE DIDACHE (reflecting church practice c. 100)**

"Concerning baptism ... baptise in running water, into the name of the Father, and of the Son, and of the Holy Spirit. But if running water is not available, then use still water; and if you cannot baptise in cold water, then use warm. But if neither is available then pour water three times upon the person's head, into the name of the Father, and Son and Holy Spirit. But before the baptism let the baptiser fast, and the baptised, and whoever else is able to: but especially instruct the baptised to fast one or two days before ... Now concerning the eucharist, give thanks in the following manner ... *(then follow a number of short prayers and responses for the bread and the cup of the eucharist)* ...

"But let no one eat or drink of your Thanksgiving except those who have been baptised into the name of the Lord; for concerning this also the Lord hath said, `Give not that which is holy to the dogs.' ... *(then follows another selection of prayers)* ...

"But you should gather yourselves together every Lord's day *(Sunday?)*, and break bread, and offer thanksgiving. But first confess all of your sins, so that your sacrifice may be pure. Let no one who is quarrelling with his fellow come together with you, unless those who are at variance are reconciled, so that your sacrifice is not profaned."

- **JUSTIN MARTYR (c. 130)**

" ... having ended the prayers, we salute one another with a kiss. There is then brought to that one of the brethren who is presiding (over the eucharist) bread and a cup of wine mixed with water; and he taking them, gives praise and glory to the Father of the universe, through the name of the Son and of the Holy Ghost, and offers thanks at considerable length for our being counted worthy to receive these things from God's hands. And when he has concluded the prayers and thanksgivings, all the people present express their assent by saying, `Amen!' ... And when the president has given thanks, and all the people have expressed their assent, those who are called by us deacons give to each of those present to partake of the bread and wine mixed with water over which thanksgiving was pronounced, and to those who are absent they carry away a portion ... And this food is called among us `eucharistia', of which no one is allowed to partake but the man who believes that the things which we teach are true, and who has been washed with the washing that is for the remission of sins ... and who is so living as Christ has enjoined. For not as common bread and common drink do we receive these; but in like manner as Jesus Christ our Saviour, having been made flesh by the word of God, had both flesh and blood for our salvation, so likewise have we been taught that the food which is blessed by the prayer of his word, and from which our flesh and blood by transmutation are nourished, is the flesh and blood of the Jesus who was made flesh ...

"And we afterwards continually remind ourselves of these things. And the wealthy among us help the needy; and we always keep together ...

"And on the day called Sunday, all who live in cities or in the country gather together to one place, and the memoirs of the apostles or the writings of the prophets are read, as long as time permits; then, when the reader has ceased, the president verbally instructs, and exhorts to the imitation of these good things. Then we all rise together and pray, and as we before said, when our prayer is ended, bread and wine and water are brought, and the president in like manner offers prayers and thanksgivings, according to his ability, and the people assent, saying "Amen!"; and there is a distribution to each, and a participation in that over which thanks have been given, and to those who are absent a portion is sent by the deacons. And they who are well-to-do and willing, give what each thinks fit; and what is collected is deposited with the president, who succours the orphans and widows, and those who, through sickness or for any other reason sojourn among us, and in a word takes care of all who are in need. But Sunday is the day on which we hold our common assembly, because ... Jesus Christ our Saviour on the same day rose from the dead ... " *(Apology 1*, Ch. 15, 16, 17).

- **CLEMENT OF ALEXANDRIA (c. 190)**

    "There are some who, in the dispensation of the eucharist...enjoin that each one of the people individually should take his part ... "

    > that is, be given a turn in handing out the elements to the congregation; of which practice Clement seems to give reluctant approval (*Miscellanies*, Bk. 1, Ch. 1)

"We hold festival, then, every day of our lives ... We cultivate our fields praising. We sail the sea, hymning ... (We are) at once grave and cheerful in all things - grave on account of the bent of the soul towards the Deity; and cheerful on account of our consideration of the blessings of humanity which God hath given us" (Ibid. Bk. 7, Ch. 7).

"So also we raise the head, and lift the hands to heaven, and set the feet in motion at the closing utterance of the prayer, following the eagerness of the spirit ... (The Christian's) whole life is a holy festival. His sacrifices are prayers, and praises, and readings in the scriptures before meals, and psalms and hymns during meals and before bed, and prayers also during the night ... " (Ibid.)

"Woman and man are to go to church decently attired, with natural step, embracing silence, possessing unfeigned love, pure in body, pure in heart, fit to pray to God. Let the woman observe this further. Let her be entirely covered, unless she happen to be at home. For that style of dress is grave, and protects from being gazed at ... (Those) who are consecrated to Christ should ... frame themselves in their whole lives (just as) they fashion themselves in the church ... (But there are those who lay) aside the inspiration of the assembly, after their departure from it, (and) they become like others with whom they associate. Nay, in laying aside the artificial mask of solemnity, they are proved to be what they secretly were. After having paid reverence to the discourse about God, they leave behind in the church what they have just heard, and outside they foolishly amuse themselves with impious playing, and amatory quavering, occupied with flute-playing, and dancing, and intoxication, and all kinds of trash..." (*The Instructor* III, Ch. 11).

" ... Let us walk worthy of the kingdom, loving God and our neighbour. But love is not proved by a kiss, but by kindly feeling. But there are those that do nothing but make the churches resound with a kiss, not having love itself within. For this very thing, the shameless use of a kiss, which ought to be mystic, occasions foul suspicions and evil reports. The apostle calls the kiss holy ... But there is another unholy kiss, full of poison, counterfeiting sanctity ... But `this is the love of God,' says John, `that we keep his commandments,' not that we stroke each other on the mouth" (Ibid.).

"Wherefore we ought to offer to God sacrifices not costly, but such as he loves ... which consist of many tongues and voices in prayer ... brought together in praises, with a pure mind, and just and right conduct ... " (Ibid. Bk. VII, Ch. 6).

"(There are sects) which have deserted the primitive church ... which employ bread and water in the oblation, not according to the canons of the church. For there are those who celebrate the eucharist with mere water ... " (*Miscellanies*, Bk. I, Ch. 20).

"But we must reject superfluous music, which enervates men's souls, and leads to variety - now mournful, and then licentious and voluptuous, and then frenzied and frantic" (Ibid. Bk. VI, Ch. 11. See also *The Instructor*, II, Ch. 4).

" ... Let us sing together simple praises, true hymns to Christ our King... O choir of peace ... O chaste people, let us celebrate on stringed instruments the God of Peace" (Ibid. Bk. III, Ch. 12).

- **MINUCIUS FELIX (c. 210)**

    concerning the cross as an object of veneration

    "Crosses, moreover, we neither worship nor wish for ... We assuredly see the sign of a cross ... when a man adores God with a pure mind, with hands outstretched ... " (*Octavius*, Ch. 29).

- **CYPRIAN (c. 240)**

    " ... Let us take also for the protection of our head the helmet of salvation ... that our bow may be fortified, so as to keep safe the sign of God (that is, of the cross) ... Let us also arm the right hand with the sword of the Spirit ... that, mindful of the eucharist, the hand which has received the Lord's body may embrace the Lord himself" (*Letter #55*).

    Note the use of the sign of the cross, and that the bread of the eucharist was received in the hand, not the mouth. Cyprian also argued that not water alone, nor wine alone, should be used in the eucharist, but water and wine mixed (*Letter #66*, para. 2, 13, 15). In para. 16 of the same letter Cyprian protests against those who were using water for a morning celebration of the eucharist, but wine in the evening. The people did this to escape persecution, for they were often recognised as Christians by the smell of wine on their breath.[89] Cyprian insisted *"we celebrate the resurrection of the Lord in the morning"*, and that wine must be used, even if that increased the chances of arrest and imprisonment.

- **THE CANONS OF THE APOSTLES (early 4th cent.)**

    "The apostles further appointed: on the first day of the week let there be service, and the reading of the holy scriptures, and the celebration of the eucharist; because on the first day of the week he ascended up to heaven, and on the first day of the week he will appear at last with the angels of heaven" (*Canon #2*).

- **THE CANONS OF HIPPOLYTUS (4th. cent.)**

    "The faithful should eat nothing before the holy communion ... Care should be taken that nothing falls from the chalice to the ground ... Women ought to be separate from the men in prayer ... Lay people

---

[89] Wine-drinking in the early morning was uncommon.

must behave soberly in church ... Let nothing fall into the sacred chalice, nor from the priests, nor from the boys when they take communion ... Let no one speak in the sanctuary, except in prayer ... When the oblations of the people cease, let the psalms be read with all attention until the signal bell is given ... "

- **THE VISION OF PAUL (4th. cent.)**

"For this cause, therefore, ye sons of men, bless the Lord unceasingly, every hour and every day; but more especially when the sun goes down; for at that hour all the angels proceed to the Lord to worship him and to present the works of men, which every man has wrought from morning till evening, whether good or evil."

- **THE APOCALYPSE OF THE VIRGIN (4th. cent.)**

" ... she saw a cloud full of fire and in it there was a multitude of men and women. And the All-Holy-One said, 'What was their sin?' And the commander-in-chief said, 'These, All-Holy-One, are they who on the morning of the Lord's day sleep like the dead, and for that reason they are chastised here' ...

"And she saw in another place burning benches of fire, and on them sat a multitude of men and women and burned on them. And the All-Holy-One asked, 'Who are these, and what is their sin?' And the commander-in-chief said, 'These, All-Holy-One, are they who did not rise up to the presbyters when they enter into the church of God ... '" (Ch. 12, 13).

Two other sources of information about the worship of the early church contain references that are too extensive for me to include in this book. But here is a summary of them -

- **TERTULLIAN (A.D. 145-220):**

    describes a worship service, including the famous jeer the pagans made against the Christians, *"See how they love each other!"* (*Apology*, Ch. 39).

    a baptismal service (*The Chaplet*, Ch. 3; also *On Baptism*, Ch. 6, 7, 8, 19, 20)

    against keeping the Jewish sabbath, and against sharing in pagan festivals (*On Idolatry*, Ch. 14).

    the public confession of sin and public discipline (*On Repentance*, Ch. 9).

    raising hands in prayer (*On Prayer*, Ch. 14, 16, 17).

    the kiss of peace (ibid. Ch. 18), and kneeling (Ch. 23).

    Sunday worship (*On Fleeing Persecution*, para. 11).

    worshipping at night during persecution (ibid. para. 14).

- **THE CONSTITUTIONS OF THE HOLY APOSTLES**

    3rd & 4th Cent.

    who may be admitted to the eucharist (Bk. 2, Sec. 5, para. 39, 40, 41).

    how the church should assemble, where each person should sit, how the service should be conducted (Bk. 2, Sec. 7; 57).

    attending church both morning and evening (para. 59).

    women must not baptise, nor laymen perform any office of the priesthood (Bk. 3, Sec. 1, para. 9, 10, 11).

    worship on Sunday, and various liturgical prayers (Bk. 7, Sec. 2, para. 30 to 38).

The above selections are either taken from, or based on, the relevant volumes in the series *"The Ante-Nicene Fathers"*, reprinted 1979 from the 19th Century edition, by Eerdmans Publishing Company, Grand Rapids, Michigan. Volume 8 of the series of 10 volumes also contains a selection of ancient liturgies dating from the 3rd and 4th centuries. They provide fascinating insights into the worship practices of the early Christians. (*See also* "The Nicene and Post-Nicene Fathers" Vol. 14, pg. 136-141, *for a discussion of later liturgical developments and of the use of special robes for the clergy - a practice that possibly reaches back as far as the 2nd. century.)*

Addendum Two

APPLAUSE

The use of applause in Christian assemblies is a thing to be treated with caution, although it has now become a common part of many charismatic/pentecostal services, not always with good purpose or good results. At the very least it could be said that no servant of Christ should thirst for personal applause, but should yearn rather to see Christ glorified.

However, if applause is spontaneously offered to a preacher or performer it should usually be accepted graciously and courteously. There is nothing to be gained by offending the people by rebuking their applause. But do not eagerly incite them to clap your performance.

The problem is not a new one, as shown by the following citations from the Fathers:

EUSEBIUS tells about Paul of Samosata, who was removed from his bishopric in 272, for many alleged crimes, including this -

> "(He) contrives to glorify himself, and deceive with appearances, and astonish the minds of the simple, preparing for himself a tribunal and lofty throne - not like a disciple of Christ ... (and) he rebukes and insults those who do not applaud and shake their handkerchiefs as in the theatres, and shout and leap about like the men and women that are stationed around him, and hear him in this unbecoming manner, but who listen reverently and orderly as in the house of God ... " (Bk. 7, Ch.30).

A better example is

CHRYSOSTOM (c. 370), he of the golden tongue, whose unequalled eloquence often drew boisterous applause. He protested vehemently against such unseemly behaviour, only to hear his very rebuke applauded! He called the hunger for applause an *"evil affection"*, and had this to say about it -

> "Many take a deal of pains to be able to stand up in public, and make a long speech; and if they get applause from the multitude, it is to them as if they gained the very kingdom (of heaven); but if silence follows the close of their speech, it is worse than hell itself, the dejection that falls upon their spirits from the silence! This has turned the Churches upside down, because you desire not to hear a discourse calculated to lead you to compunction, but one that may delight you from the sound and composition of the words, as though you were listening to singers and minstrels; and we too act a preposterous and pitiable part in being led by your lusts, when we ought to root them out ...
>
> "Believe me, I speak no other than I feel - when as I discourse I hear myself applauded, at the moment indeed I feel it as a man (for why should I not own the truth?); I am delighted and give way to the pleasurable feeling; but when I get home, and bethink me that those who applauded received no benefit from my discourse, but that whatever benefit they ought to have got, they lost it while applauding and praising, I am in pain, and groan, and weep, and feel as if I had spoken all in vain ... Nay, often have I thought to make a rule which should prevent all applauding, and persuade you to listen with silence and becoming orderliness ... What means that noise again? I am laying down a rule against this very thing, and you have not the forbearance even to hear me?" (The people had begun to applaud his suggestion of a rule against applause! *Homily* 30, on *The Acts of the Apostles*, Acts 13:42).

On another occasion Chrysostom was demanding that the people rise up and *"chastise the blasphemers"* that were troubling the church, when he was interrupted by prolonged applause. He complained -

> "What need have I of these plaudits, these cheers, these tumultuous signs of approval? The praise I seek is that ye show forth all I have said in your works. Then am I an enviable and happy man, not when ye approve, but when ye perform with all readiness, whatsoever ye hear

> from me!" (*Homilies on the Statutes* 2:12. See also *Homily* 5:21; and 7:10).

At the end of a singularly eloquent exposition of Romans 8:28, he was constrained to make the same protest -

> "What is the good of these applauses and clamours? I demand one thing only of you, and that is the display of them in real action, the obedience of deeds. This is my praise, this is your gain, this gives me more lustre than a diadem!" (*Homilies on Romans 15*: Conclusion. See also the conclusion of his *Homily 5 on 1 Corinthians*. And for a more extended presentation of Chrysostom's views on applause, and on those who seek it, see his work *On The Priesthood* 5:1, 2, 3, 8).

(The passages quoted come from The Nicene and Post-Nicene Fathers, First Series, "Saint Chrysostom;" a 1978 reprint by the W. B. Eerdmans Publishing Company of the 19th century volumes.)

Addendum Three

SOME SCRAPS OF PERSONAL PREJUDICE

Here are some further comments, perhaps expressing personal prejudice as much as biblical doctrine, about the boisterous worship style that some charismatic/pentecostal churches in our day have adopted. They are often prone also to advocate "dancing before the Lord", by which is usually meant a free skipping up and down, a kind of spontaneous and unstructured two-step.

OUTDOOR PRAISE

Have you ever thought of this? There were two quite separate worship expressions in ancient Israel:

in the temple, where worship was mostly formal, liturgical, and professional; and

outdoors, in the great annual festivals, and other national and local celebrations, which were clamorous, exuberant, improvised - more akin to what we today would call a "folk festival" or "carnival".

Many references to worship in the OT belong to the second aspect, not the first, and therefore are hardly transferable to the church.

THE APOCALYPSE

Some people support the case for ebullient worship by citing the several references to collective and noisy praise that occur in the *Apocalypse*. They quote those scriptures, and then exhort the church to worship the Lord more vociferously. But here is something for you to ponder: public worship is not strongly emphasised in the NT letters; indeed, major passages on loud worship exist only in the *Apocalypse*. The apostles apparently saw collective praise as more a **heavenly** act than an **earthly** one.

The reasons are obvious.

There have been many times in the history of the church when extroverted congregational worship was impossible, when vigorous and public praise would have brought instant imprisonment or death.

It follows then, that while collective worship is obviously desirable and enjoyable, and while heartfelt praise can be a source of spontaneous church growth, it is not essential for vital spiritual life. But fellowship, teaching, and mutual exhortation, are certainly essential - yet they can be done quietly (if necessary) and privately.

POWERFUL PRAISE?

Such passages as *Acts 16:16-26* are sometimes quoted as proof that vigorous praise has power to fling open the prison doors of life. No doubt lively praise has often achieved just that effect. Yet in *Acts* the Philippi incident was the only time praise did succeed in throwing open a prison. Later, when Paul was again imprisoned (this time for several years), he had to wear his chains patiently. Indeed, he experienced the embarrassment of having to write from prison to the same Philippians from whose jail he had once been supernaturally rescued! The efficacy of praise to change one's environment is plainly restricted by various factors, not least among them the larger purpose of God.

ON NOISY PRAISE

I have often heard it said that God is restoring to the church today the original pattern of praise and worship, which (it is claimed) was exuberant, noisy, spontaneous, and demonstrative. Such a boisterous worship style is then adversely contrasted with main-stream traditional worship, which is restrained, dignified, and formal.

How biblical are those claims?

It is true, as I have mentioned above, that Israel's outdoor celebrations, her folk festivals, were exuberant; but the highly liturgical structure of many of the Psalms, the ornate ritual prescribed for the priests, the existence of professional choristers, dancers, and musicians, all suggest a much more formal approach in the Temple.

Presumably the same was true of synagogue worship, which provided the model for the early church. In any case, the worship practices of national Israel are not automatically transferable to the universal church. Unlike Israel, the church has to temper its worship performance to the circumstances in which it finds itself.

ON PAUL

I doubt that Paul would be comfortable with, or much enjoy, the raucous revelry that characterises the worship of some modern pentecostal churches. He certainly would not find it familiar, and probably would not find it congenial. The high theology and great dignity of the few lines of poetry and/or hymns scattered through the NT suggest a rather sober style of worship (cp. 1 Timothy 1:17; 6:15-16; Philippians 2:5-11; Ephesians 1:3-14; Romans 8:31-39; 1 Corinthians 13:4-7).

Have you ever read the church Fathers on worship? Quite early in the growth of the church elaborate liturgies came into common use. It is difficult to deny that those liturgies must have had some real connection with apostolic practice. Such a radical and rapid departure from the first traditions of the church would be improbable.

My personal preference, I must admit (even if it is just a mark of advancing age!), is for a more structured and formal liturgy. I endure rather than enjoy some of the worship sessions I am obliged to attend. I yearn from time to time to participate in a majestic hymn sung majestically, to hear a fine chorale, to be stirred by a powerful and well-performed cantata, to delight in a sweet motet, to be aroused to worship by walking into the sanctuary to the sound of a thrilling Bach prelude, to be drawn into the eucharist by an irresistible Purcell introit, to feel that the angels are blending their voices with a glorious anthem sung by the chancel choir, to exit the house of God with the magnificent strains of a splendid postlude reverberating around me!

Instead, I am too often obliged to suffer patiently the ear-sundering thump of some of the crassest worship music ever written, and some of the most superficial and rowdy worship practices ever performed. If I thought heaven had nothing better to offer, I would despair. Happily, I am persuaded that the madly beaten drums, the cacophonously played guitars, and the wildly overamplified racket that sometimes assaults my ears will be absent at least from *my* corner of Paradise! Surely there must be others who, like myself, find it almost impossible to relate with any pleasure to the raucous worship practised in some churches? We lovers of dignity, grace, and musical excellence in public worship may be a minority, but the Lord still likes us!

Part Three

THE WORSHIP LEADER

Chapter Eleven

LOOKING AT YOURSELF!

I once heard it said, "*When giants are mentioned in the Bible they are always on the side of the enemy*." That may not be quite true, for Paul declared that God does:

> *... call a few who are powerful, wise, and noble (1 Corinthians 1:26)*.

Yet it remains clear that God more often chooses what is foolish in the world to shame the wise, and what is weak in the world to shame the strong

> *... so that no human being can boast in the presence of God (1 Corinthians 1:27-29)*.

If you are among the latter group (that is, among the many worship leaders who are not strongly gifted, rather than among the few who are) then this chapter should help to make you more effective. It deals with the way you should look at yourself and at your audience. I encourage you to meditate on the following maxims -

YOUR PERSONAL ATTITUDE

SELF-RESPECT

If you do not respect yourself, do not expect the audience to respect you.

- Convey self-respect by your manner, by the way you dress, speak, and move, and by the attitude you expect others to have toward you.
- You will, of course, know the difference between self-respect, and conceit or vanity.

GOOD HUMOUR

If you cannot endure to be laughed at, stay off the platform.

♦ Anyone who regularly stands on a platform is bound to make mistakes and to become an object of laughter.

You must be able to laugh at your own errors, and to accept the laughter of others with good humour. Let me repeat what I have said before: you should not take either yourself or your ministry too seriously. Of course, what you are doing is important; but you must keep a sense of proportion. Be honest now, do you really think the security of the kingdom of God was endangered by those mistakes you made last Sunday? Is the Lord really so dependent upon you doing just the right thing? A hundred years from now, will anyone even know, let alone care, whether or not you were a success?

> It will be all the same in a hundred years -
> What a spell-word to conjure up smiles and tears!
> How oft do I muse, 'mid the thoughtless and gay,
> On the marvellous truth that those words convey!
>
> For Time, as he speeds on invisible wings,
> Disenamels and withers earth's costliest things.
> And the knight's white plume, and the shepherd's crook,
> And the minstrel's pipe, and the scholar's book,
> And the emperor's crown, and his Cossack's spears,
>
> Will be dust alike in a hundred years![90]
>
> Soon fades the spell, soon comes the night;
> Say will it not be then the same,
> Whether we played the black or white,
> Whether we lost or won the game?[91]

---

[90] In A Hundred Years, attributed to Elizabeth Doten; stanza one and the latter half of stanza three (out of six stanzas)

[91] Sermon In A Churchyard, stanza eight; Lord Macauley. When he was only four hot coffee was spilled on his legs. Lady Waldegrave asked him how he was feeling and he replied, "Thank you, madam, the agony is abated."

- Be content to be happy when you succeed, not too distraught when you fail, and always able to stand off to one side and look at yourself, and chuckle.
- We only make ourselves absurd if we become too self-important or too earnest, not able to see ourselves as we really are.

Be willing to be laughed at

If you, my reader, are a male, what would you do if one of the ladies in the congregation came up to you in the middle of a hymn and whispered, "Your fly is undone"? That happened to me once! I casually moved to a less conspicuous position, waited until the hymn was ended, called the congregation to prayer, and when every head was safely bowed, made the necessary adjustment. To this day I don't know whether anyone except her noticed that open zipper. I am happy to remain in ignorance!

Or what would you do if, in mid-sermon, at a point of singular passion and eloquence, your false teeth flew out and went clacking across the floor? That happened to a friend of mine. He paused, shared the laughter of the people, picked up his teeth, dusted and replaced them, and quickly got back into his message.

Another friend of mine who lost his teeth managed to catch them in midair and sweep them back into his mouth so quickly the people didn't have time to laugh. He behaved with such perfect poise, most of them weren't even sure what had happened. Indeed, he continued his sermon as though nothing had happened.

I once watched while another preacher, in the enthusiasm of his message, stepped too far and fell right off the platform. He had been trained in the army how to jump out of a rapidly moving vehicle and roll so that he would not be injured. And that is exactly what he did. He hit the floor, rolled, was back on his feet in a moment, and continued to preach from floor level as though that is exactly what he had intended to do. It was the most amazing exercise in self-control I have ever seen!

Try to develop the same kind of unflappability.

SINCERITY

The chief virtue, the brightest shield, the finest strength of a worship leader is sincerity; a sham, a show-off, will soon be discovered and scorned by the people.

Milton was wrong when he said

> "neither man nor angel can discern hypocrisy, the only evil that walks invisible except to God alone."

A hypocrite on the public platform will soon be discovered. So heed the advice of Sirach and

> "do not winnow in every wind, nor walk along every path, for this is the mark of duplicity. Stand firmly by what you know, and be consistent in what you say (5:9-10)

Yet the admonition to be sincere seems to be insincere. Surely it is a pretence to strive for sincerity? That depends on how "sincerity" is defined. Sincerity is certainly more than just doing what comes naturally; it is more than acting upon every impulse that stirs in your mind - although I have often seen such behaviour defended in the name of sincerity.

The great Chinese philosopher Chu Hsi (1130-1200) taught that a state of sincerity is reached when a person manages to strike a mean between deficiency and excess; that is, when one does in each situation neither more nor less than is proper. That seems to be a fair definition. It is close to Paul's injunction that we should

> "let our moderation be observed by all men" (Philippians 4:5).

There is an old idea that "sincerity" comes from two Latin words meaning "without wax" - for wax was used to disguise imperfections in marble statuary. Hence the work of a sculptor who used no wax would be free from cracks or blemishes; but a waxed statue was not what it seemed to be. According to Partridge that idea has been discarded, and it is now thought that "sincere" comes from the Latin "sincerus", meaning pure - that is, unmixed with any foreign substance. A sincere person is genuine. He does not pretend to be what he is not. Deceitfulness is abhorrent to him. He is frank and natural.

Yet absolute frankness and raw nature are hardly acceptable on the platform. Sincerity does not require brutal honesty so much as freedom from moral corruption and verbal falsehood. Courtesy, gentle manners, gracious restraint, are hardly enemies of sincerity.

But most of all, for a Christian, sincerity means bringing one's conduct and conversation into alignment with scripture. Hence an Act of Parliament in the time of King Henry VIII spoke about "the sincere and pure doctrine of Goddes Worde". With complete sincerity a Christian may always affirm what scripture says. We may be actual sinners, but we can always declare ourselves righteous in Christ. Any Christian can boldly pronounce himself to be everything scripture says he is. There is no insincerity in that, unless the affirmation itself is insincere, that is, lacking in faith.

The audience will reflect the manner of the leader

CONFIDENCE

Fear is your greatest enemy; confidence your best friend.

- An audience will not easily forgive you if you distress it by standing on the platform displaying a bad case of nervous jitters.

Any show of personal embarrassment, or of painful self-consciousness, will make the people feel uncomfortable, and may actually offend them.

So if a situation arises that could embarrass you, act quickly to take the tension out of the meeting. Never stand there stricken or dismayed.

Relax the people by letting them know you are not about to fall apart; you still have yourself and the situation under control. If laughter is an appropriate response then let the people know they can safely laugh at you by heartily sharing and enjoying their amusement.

- ◆ Nervousness, an attitude of insecurity, unconsciously convey to the people a set of messages that discredit your right to be on the platform.

Your audience may interpret your nervousness in several negative ways -

- ◆ "I am afraid I will fail because I lack the skills to do this job well"
- ◆ then you should not have gone onto the platform until you had developed at least the minimal skills needed to perform your task acceptably.
- ◆ "I am too proud to face the humiliation that will engulf me if I fail."
- ◆ in that case you have forfeited your right to public leadership.
- ◆ "I am afraid of the people, that they will not respond to my direction."
- ◆ so you have turned the people into enemies, and they may respond as you expect them to.
- ◆ "I am a nervous person, I can't change, so you will just have to endure this jittery performance."
- ◆ but perhaps God has not called you to a public ministry; or perhaps you are just failing to find strength in his grace.

However on this matter of nervousness, you should realise a few important things:

- ◆ Some public performers never overcome their nervousness; others do so only in familiar situations; but they all learn to make constructive use of their nervousness.

- Nervousness should be your friend, not your enemy; the very force that might immobilise you in fear can be changed into a source of dynamic energy.
- All power comes out of a state of tension, and tightly strung nerves are a good source of that tension.

Indeed, if you were not at all nervous, to avoid being flaccid you would have to find another way to inject energy into your performance. So don't try to fight nervous tension, or to rid yourself of it, but use it to put life, strength, sparkle, into your ministry. If you do so, you will find that the moment you begin to speak you will quite forget you were nervous.

I should add that there are two kinds of nervousness: positive, caused by the stimulus of a new environment, a fresh challenge, an unfamiliar situation; and negative, caused by a sense of inadequacy, or based on poor preparation for the task. Only the first kind can be turned into a source of energy; the second is destructive, and if you are doing a God-given work and have properly fitted yourself for the task, you should never suffer from it.

AUTHORITY

The people will not grant you any more authority than you claim yourself.

- They may not even allow you as much authority as you assert; and they will certainly not yield you any more!
- So you should convey to the audience, by your manner and bearing, your confidence, that they will accept your authority as the leader of the meeting.

Give firm, clear instructions, without apology, with never a thought that the people might not do as you ask.

- Generally speaking, an audience will reflect the manner, character, and purpose of the leader.

If you are nervous, unsure of yourself, ill-prepared, lacking in aim and direction, this will have an unsettling effect on the people. But if you are confident (or at least appear to be so), relaxed, friendly, purposeful, the audience will naturally respond in the same way.

- If you know that God has given you the task of leading the people, or of ministering to them, then seize that role boldly, without apology, without false humility.

You should stand in the sure sense that behind you stands the authority of Christ himself. But never forget: confidence, authority, forcefulness, must be qualified by a genuine inner humility. The people will be quickly repelled by a leader who conveys a sense of carnal pride or of arrogance.

NATURAL

A worship leader who assumes an artificial manner of behaving or speaking will hinder the people from discovering reality in worship.

- Be as human and as natural as possible in the way you conduct yourself on the platform.

Many leaders adopt an artificial and often ridiculous tone of voice or style of speaking. They assume a kind of "pious" intonation or phraseology. When they lead in prayer they use a "sing-song" voice - probably in an effort to convey the idea of emotion, or of spiritual power. But when there is real cause for emotion there is no need to simulate it; and power in prayer comes not from noise, nor from a false tremolo, but from praying in harmony with the will of God, in faith. Avoid like the plague any kind of artificiality or pretence. You fool no one but yourself.

- Avoid peppering your speech with "glory", "hallelujah", "praise God", and the like.

Use such expressions terms only when their use is truly meaningful. Used casually or carelessly they become religious jargon, evangelical slang, Pentecostal profanity. Indeed, some Christians, in their thoughtless and constant use of pious exclamations, make themselves more truly profane than their ungodly neighbours are.

- Speak simply and directly, cutting out roundabout speaking (what is known as circumlocution).

If you love the people, you will not play games with them.

It is amazing how many people, when they get on a platform, suddenly feel there is something indecent about a direct statement. So they develop all kinds of indirect ways of saying things. If they cannot avoid a direct statement, they must still disguise it behind a thicket of qualifiers, and a forest of verbiage. They are as apologetic as the man of whom William Cowper wrote:

> He would not, with a peremptory tone,
> Assert the nose upon his face his own.

Sir Ernest Gowers has this comment on roundabout speech -

"No doubt it comes partly from a feeling that wordiness is an ingredient of politeness, and blunt statement is crude, if not rude. There is an element of truth in this: an over-staccato style is as irritating as an over-sostenuto one ... Moreover the habit of `padding' springs partly from less meritorious notions - that the dignity of an official's calling demands a certain verbosity, and that naked truth is indecent and should be clothed in wrappings of woolly words"[92]

So, when a simple "No!" is called for, never say, "The reply is in the negative!"

MANNERISMS

"A preacher who has a hundred virtues obscures all with one fault."

- That aphorism is from Martin Luther, who also said -

    "Nothing is seen more easily and quickly in preachers than their faults ... Dr Jonas has all the virtues of a good preacher, but people cannot overlook the fact that the good man clears his throat so frequently"[93]

- The delivery of many preachers, the performance of many worship leaders, is marred by some annoying flaw that robs their ministry of its power.

---

[92] The Complete Plain Words, pg 98-99. Here are some other examples, from Fowler: instead of "no news is good news", the circumlocution "the absence of intelligence is an indication of satisfactory developments"; instead of "the men have no vote", the circumlocution, "participation by the men in the control of the industry is non-existent". Or consider these: "we face an absolute dearth of fiscal supply" for "we have no money"; or, "the penultimate month of the year" for "November"; or, "the elimination with extreme prejudice of the intelligence agency operative" for "the spy was shot.

[93] What Luther Says, Vol 3, pg 110.

They have developed mannerisms that rivet the attention of the people and distract them from the Word and from worship. David McCarthy warns against mannerisms like these:

- frequently rubbing an ear, nose, or the top of your head
- fixing a smile on your face (which may cause your audience to doubt your sincerity)
- fixing a frown on your face (which may give an impression of belligerence)
- never looking the people in the eye
- folding and unfolding your hands
- pulling out and replacing a handkerchief
- frequently shifting your glasses
- putting your hands in and out of your pocket
- cramped and nervous movements
- fiddling with items that are on the pulpit.[94]

To those I would add some other often observed habits: buttoning and unbuttoning a coat; constantly hitching up trousers; frequent sips of water; fondling coat lapels; and the like.

YOUR PUBLIC ATTITUDE

One word describes the constant attitude you should have toward your audience: respect. The following precepts describe some of the ingredients of that respect. Ponder them carefully.

SERVICE

You are the servant of the people of God, not their lord.

- Your first act of respect for the people, when you step up to the pulpit or microphone, should be a courteous greeting.

---

[94] From an article in "Christianity Today", date unknown to me

- Arrange your paper, books Bible, etc., after you have greeted the people.

They can hardly escape an impression that you are self-centred, or that you consider things more important than you consider them, or that you are just plain rude, if you do not bother to greet them until a minute or two after you have arrived at the podium. The people may reciprocate such discourtesy by declining to give you their full attention.

GRACIOUSNESS

Keep an easy manner, and cultivate graciousness in your bearing and speech.

- A natural, winsome, pleasant approach, will elicit the greatest response from an audience; you can maintain intensity, energy, and drive without becoming wrought up and agitated.

- Be enthusiastic, but not excitable; forceful, but not overbearing; cheerful, but not flippant; vigorous, but not rowdy; lively, but not boisterous; strong, but not domineering; dynamic, but not aggressive.

- Wildly extravagant behaviour, boorishness, flippancy, indifference, fanaticism, emotion for emotion's sake (that is, without proper cause), all show disrespect for the people, and in most cases will produce a negative response.

I have been irritated by preachers who have an astonishing ability to produce tears whenever they choose. Now their cheeks are wet with deep grief; a few moments later they are laughing merrily; but wait a minute and they will again be consumed with grief. I remember one such man whose tears were so easily formed that it became quite offensive. I remember not one word he said; but the memory of those tears that came and went so easily has stuck in my mind like a burr. Emotion (whether of joy or sorrow) for which there is an adequate cause will not be disturbing. But the people will resist the manipulative use of artificially aroused emotion.

TACT

The full confidence of a crowd is gained with difficulty; yet it can be lost easily, and you may not be able to regain it.

- ♦ So be careful not to offend the people, either thoughtlessly or deliberately; tact is most important; try not to say a word out of place.
- ♦ Never, never, speak rudely or offensively to your audience, for if you do, they will hardly forgive you.

You may rebuke them from scripture for some kind of spiritual or moral failure; but you have no right to rebuke them merely for failure to cooperate in the conduct of the meeting. It is your task to win their eager cooperation. If you have to bully or berate them, you have already failed in that task. Petulance or aggrieved pride is inexcusable on the platform.

- ♦ Be careful in the use of humour; remember that many people are disturbed by mother-in-law jokes,[95] ethnic jokes, or insulting remarks about one's spouse, and the like.
- ♦ Be especially careful in linking humour with holy or serious things. There is often a fine line between humour and sacrilege.

Furthermore, audiences do not always respond in the same way to a particular piece of humour; much depends upon the mood of the crowd (see the discussion of "mood" in the next chapter).

SENSITIVITY

Do you love and respect the people? Then you will remain sensitive at all times to their reactions.

- ♦ If you see that you are getting a bad response, swiftly change what you are saying or doing.

---

[95] This, for example, is one other thing I remember about the preacher who offended me with his phony tears. He had a propensity for cracking insulting jokes. I happen to love my mother-in-law, who is a truly wonderful lady. This crass preacher told this so-called joke: "I have some good news, and some bad news. The bad news - your car went off the road, down a cliff, and pulverised on some rocks. The good news - your mother-in-law was driving it." I was not amused, and I still have no recollection of his sermon, but I can remember being annoyed by that "joke".

- If you have offended the people, apologise.
- Take the blame yourself for mistakes the people make.

If the mistake is yours, do not distress the people by standing there in a blushing quandary. Make some light comment that eases everybody. Tension in a meeting is an enemy of your purpose.

- Once again, remember that an audience dislikes being embarrassed. If you hurt, or trouble, or offend the people, you may find it impossible to regain their confidence.
- A good worship leader will be constantly aware of the people.

He will never just stand there worshipping God by himself, lost in the glory of the Lord. He knows it is his task to set an excellent example of worship, but he will blend into his own worship constant encouragement of the people.

- A good worship leader will not fall behind the people in his devotion and worship of God, but neither will he press too far ahead of them.

If they are not responding to his example, he will pause to find the reason, and patiently begin again to bring them to the level of worship he (or she) desires.

- If the people are tardy in their response, his respect for them will prevent a good worship leader from being critical or caustic.

He will not be like the man who cried out in exasperation, "What's the matter with you people? A choir of crows with croup would sing with more melody!" A good worship leader will always prefer, and will succeed with, kindness and courtesy.

So be governed by good sense in what you do on the platform. Stir up in yourself love and respect for the people. Maintain a relaxed and pleasant manner. Approach your task with confidence in Christ and in yourself. Keep attuned to your audience, being always sensitive to their needs and flexible enough at any time to change your programme.

Do those things, and you will be well on the way toward helping the people to enjoy a beautiful worship experience.

Chapter Twelve

PLATFORM TECHNIQUE

This chapter deals with the practical aspects of running a meeting and of directing the music and singing. Nothing here requires you to be a professional musician, nor a skilled orator. Even if your abilities are quite modest, you should be able to absorb and utilise the following ideas.

BASIC PRINCIPLES

Keep your technique as inoffensive and as unobtrusive as possible.

- ♦ Nobody is offended by grace, dignity, good dress, good manners, good speech, and so on; but the opposite does offend many people (cp. 1 Corinthians 14:40).

- ♦ However, people do not want the dignity of a mausoleum; it is better to have life with a little confusion than the ordered peace of a graveyard. (Which is more appealing to the eye and heart: children at play, or a cemetery?)

BEGIN WITH THE PEOPLE

You can do almost anything you like with a crowd, if you begin where the people are and take them on from there.

- ♦ Often a worship leader will bounce onto the platform, launch into a vigorous song, and expect the people in a few moments to reach the pitch of excitement or joy that is motivating him; instead, he is likely to achieve an opposite effect.

You must at least begin where the people are, take them by the hand, and then carefully lead them to where they should be. But before you can do that you must know the answer to two questions -

First: "What kind of a crowd am I facing?"

Is it a *foreign* crowd (the people are mostly strangers to each other); or a friendly crowd (they share a common interest, but do not all know each other); or a familiar crowd (they not only share a common interest but are all good friends)? The first kind you might find in, say, a city-wide evangelistic crusade; the second, in a large local church; the third, in a smaller local church or a home fellowship. Each of those audiences requires a different approach in order to achieve the desired result.

Second: "What mood is the crowd in?"

Are the people noisy, quiet, responsive, restless, aloof, eager, sober, indifferent, involved, sad, joyful, and so on? The mood of a crowd is a result of the blending of the diverse moods of each individual. A host of influences have been at work shaping those emotions. For that reason, the mood of a crowd is usually unpredictable. The same group of people, meeting in the same church, may display a different mood week by week. So you cannot just assume that the lively opening song that was a great success last Sunday will have the same effect this Sunday. It might in fact get the same rough reception as the man got who tried to sell smog to Sydney.

- ♦ The answers to those questions will determine how you should begin the meeting, what is permissible in the conduct of the meeting, how rapidly you can advance the meeting toward the goal that has been set, and so on.

You plainly have more freedom of action when facing a "familiar" crowd than when you are facing a "*foreign*" one; or, when the mood of the crowd is, say, responsive rather than diffident.

CHANGING THEIR MOOD

Do not take liberties with the emotions of the people, for they will not readily forgive you.

- ♦ In every crowd there is potential goodwill toward the leader; normally they are not thinking of obstructing your programme.

But they are not obliged to like you, nor to obey you. It is your task to sell yourself to the people and to make them eager to follow you.

- For example, the people do not have to sing; they may not be in a singing mood.

Your task is to make them want to sing, and then to see that they thoroughly enjoy singing.

- If you trespass against their mood, and try to force them to do what they do not yet feel like doing, you will simply turn their mood into one of stubborn resistance.

Even if, out of politeness, they cooperate with you, their actions will lack heart and warmth.

You can change the mood of a crowd; but you must first get in tune with it, and go along with it, and then you can tactfully change it.

- You should begin by adopting an attitude and choosing a song, reading, or other worship activity that is sympathetic with their present mood.
- You can put together a combination of prayers, songs, readings, and the like that will bring the people to the required mood or response (see below under "Music Technique").

BEFORE THE MEETING

You are called to serve God with your mind, as well as your spirit.

- Which means there is a place in the conduct of a meeting, not only for the immediate inspiration of the Holy Spirit, but also for careful preparation.

As Aesop said in the moral to his fable "The Ant and the Grasshopper" - "It is thrifty to prepare today for the wants of tomorrow."

- During the meeting you should, of course, remain open to intervention by the Holy Spirit, and to his spontaneous leading; but it is absurd to suppose that the Spirit can guide you only during the meeting.

Surely it is more likely that clear guidance can be obtained when you are praying at home, free from the distractions of the public environment?

- Generally, you should aim to be as well prepared as you can: the programme planned, the songs chosen, the musician(s) organised, the announcements ready, the furniture arranged, etc.

Keep the platform as tidy and as uncluttered as possible.

- ♦ If you hold to a theology of Christ being present in the preaching of the Word, then you will seek to remove everything that might distract the eye or attention of the people.

So it is undesirable to have pictures or banners behind the preacher. The best background is a plain soft-hued drape. It is best not to have other people on the platform during the sermon; arrange for them to join the congregation when the preacher takes over.

"It is not enough to do good; one must do it in the right way."[96]

Good intentions are no excuse for a lazy performance. In the service of Christ, near enough is not good enough.

- ♦ If you have the authority to do so, then demand from all who are going to participate in the meeting - in song, Bible reading, prayer, or musical performance - the very best they can do.
- ♦ Insist that vocal soloists memorise their words, and that instrumental soloists memorise their music, and that all musical items are well practised.

Do not allow lack-lustre performances. Do not allow a slovenly approach to any form of platform ministry. Think for a moment about what you have seen on T.V. Even little children, under the spotlights, facing the cameras, singing secular songs, do so from memory, with immense verve.

No one ever holds a piece of paper in his hand. So remain firm against any pressure to allow a lesser standard in the church. The service of Christ demands the best the people can give.

---

[96] John, Viscount Morley of Blackburn.

If you are sitting on the platform, stay alert and interested.

DURING THE MEETING

As the platform party is, so will be the congregation.

- ♦ If you are not leading the meeting, but have to be on the platform, do not slouch, but sit gracefully.

Try not to distract the people by unnecessary movements. Even if the proceedings are insufferably dreary, at least appear to be interested!

Other people may be fascinated with what is being said and done and you owe them (and the speaker) the courtesy of not undermining their interest.

Watch the people carefully, and make sure you have not left them behind.

- Give them time to find the song or Bible reading before continuing with the meeting.
- Encourage audience participation by giving clear instructions.

When you want the people to stand, indicate this with your hands as well as your voice. Don't hesitate to announce the number of a song, or a scripture reference, several times if necessary.

Keep the people more aware of God than of themselves.

- Avoid long silences, during which the people become steadily more self- conscious and keenly aware of even the slightest noise.
- Don't keep them either standing or sitting for too long, thus causing their sense of God to be overcome by their physical discomfort.
- Don't allow the auditorium to be too hot or too cold.
- Throughout the meeting watch the people and notice what is happening among them. Observe their responses and reactions.

Are they showing signs of restlessness and weariness? Change direction before the mood of the whole meeting is adversely affected.

Have they been standing so long that many of them are beginning to sit down of their own accord? Quickly seat those who are still standing before they are all infected with rebellion! (You will not, of course, growl at those who sat down prematurely. The fault was not theirs, but yours, for wearying them.)

Is their enthusiasm for song waning? Don't try to stir them up to new endeavour. Let them rest while you read a passage of scripture, or lead them in prayer, or invite some testimonies. When they are refreshed they will sing with a new vigour.

Forget at your own peril that people are creatures of habit.

- ♦ You should take the initiative in varying the pattern of the services from time to time; but remember that people do not like, and will resist, sudden and arbitrary change.

- ♦ Heed the wisdom of Mark Twain - "Habit is habit, and not to be flung out the window by any man, but coaxed downstairs a step at a time."

So if you do alter the usual order of service, prepare the people beforehand; give a reason for the alteration; do nothing without a beneficial purpose, stated or implied.

True worship will be three things: emotional, intelligent, and spiritual.

- ♦ Seek to structure the service so that the people can bring their whole being (body, soul, and spirit) into the act of worship.

If the people have no idea what is to happen next it is difficult for them to give a complete response. It is true in worship as elsewhere, "There is no more miserable human being than one in whom nothing is habitual but indecision" (William James).

A worship programme built around constant uncertainty and surprise will never advance beyond shallow emotional excitement. Such a programme cannot exercise fully the minds of the people, nor can it plumb the depths of their spirits.

- ♦ Despite the above, there may be occasions when a desired effect can best be achieved by a sudden innovation: but let your every action be controlled by discretion.

Never apologise for who you are or what you are, nor for the task you have been given.

- ♦ Don't even apologise if you are ill-equipped; and on no account confess that you are ill-prepared.

If you are not fitted for the task the people will discover it soon enough, and there will always be some who won't notice - so why disillusion them?

If you are ill prepared the people will soon discover it

THE USE OF "PLOYS"

Note: I have searched diligently to find a suitable word to describe the various special activities that worship leaders often ask audiences to perform (that is, such things as clapping; embracing; men or women singing; greeting each other; and the like). I have finally settled upon "ploy" - which among other things means an action contrived to achieve a certain purpose. A "contrived" action is one that would not have happened naturally, but has been introduced into the scene.

Other possible choices were "stunts" or "gimmicks", but they are emotively negative when associated with worship; and I rejected words like "activities" because they are applicable to the whole worship service, not just to the special items I am using "ploy" to define.

Use ploys with great discretion, according to the size of the crowd and its mood, and the purpose of the meeting.

- ♦ Remember that an embarrassed or irritated person is one for whom the rest of the meeting will be largely futile.

People dislike any attack on their normal social inhibitions.

- ♦ So you should be careful before introducing any ploy that goes beyond the bounds of ordinary behaviour.

For example: "Turn around and shake hands with three people and tell them that you love them!" Many people dislike being forced into promiscuous contact with strangers, or even with acquaintances. They prefer to reserve such intimacies for close friends, and they resent being asked to squander their privacy.[97] Not everyone enjoys being effusively greeted, hugged, or kissed by strangers (or even by friends). They may feel that such displays are superficial, and that they trivialise love.

- ♦ Beware of assuming that because a certain action offends you, or pleases you, it will have the same effect on everyone; not everybody is an extrovert, nor an introvert.

Hence, there are many people, the opposite of those mentioned above, who thoroughly enjoy an opportunity to cast aside normal reserves, and just for a few moments to revel in a feeling that all of the people are one loving family - no barriers, no grudges, no envies, just friendship and affection. To them the church is a place where they can forget artificial social restraints and taboos, and worship God without inhibition, clapping, dancing, singing, rejoicing - things they cannot do at home, or at work, but only in the church.

---

[97] Have you noticed, in a crowded elevator, how persistently people try to keep some private "space" around themselves, even to the extent of avoiding eye contact with their fellow passengers, and certainly, if at all possible, preventing any physical contact.

- The key is to know beforehand whether the theme of the meeting, and the nature of the crowd, require an introverted or an extroverted approach.

Whichever it is, at least some people in the audience will initially be out of sympathy with that approach. But by proper preparation you can so shape the meeting that eventually everyone will be willing to participate heartily in whatever the programme demands.

- But if there are some who still decline to participate in a ploy you should allow them the freedom in Christ to refuse.

Encouragement to participate should not slide into coercion. Nor should any inference be allowed that the Christian faith or zeal of those who do not want to participate is suspect. Nothing in scripture obliges anyone to perform a ploy against their will, or to violate their deeply felt social restraints.

Several years ago "dancing in the Spirit" was a new idea that swept across the country. In some places worship leaders declared that people who declined to dance were spiritually "bound", that unless they danced they would never find real spiritual freedom. There were others (including myself) who were equally adamant that we had no need of a two-step in the aisle to prove that we were liberated. We saw that in Christ we already had freedom, to dance or not to dance, as we deemed best. Those other coercive leaders were actually robbing many people of their true liberty.

It is a mistake to use ploys to bring about a friendly or relaxed atmosphere.

- More times than I care to remember I have seen violence done to people's feelings by worship leaders who think the meeting is "slow", so they decide to liven it with some ploy.

For example: shake hands with, or hug, so many people; tell so many people they are beautiful and God loves them; get out in the aisles and dance before the Lord; stand up and clap loudly; those over 30 sing against those under 30; wave your Bibles in the air and shout "Praise God!"; and the like.

Now any one of those actions may have been successful on another occasion, or even at a different point in the same meeting; but at the time they were introduced they were discordant. They ravaged the social restraints of many of the people; especially of the shy and the more sensitive.

- ◆ The rule is: you can use almost any ploy after the crowd is relaxed and ready for it, but not before.

Not everyone enjoys being hugged by a stranger!

Introduce a ploy too soon, and you will force the people to withdraw into themselves, to put up internal barriers against further invasions of their privacy and integrity - barriers they may hold in place for the rest of the meeting, not only against the worship leader, but also against the preacher. Instead of preparing people to be open to the word of God, I have seen many worship leaders cause them to blockade themselves against the word. Self-defence against an ill-mannered attack upon one's emotions and sensibilities is an instinctive and powerful reaction. The worship leader who ignores that reaction will probably create an atmosphere detrimental both to true worship and to a ready response to the scriptures.

- Out of politeness, or because of peer pressure, or the fear of being further embarrassed, people may sometimes obey the leader's command and do things they dislike.

But while their faces may be smiling, many of them "freeze" inside, so that during the remainder of the meeting they refuse to give anything more than a polite or superficial response. A wise leader will therefore heed this dictum -Use ploys only when the mood of the people ensures they will be successful.

- If the starting atmosphere of the meeting is formal, "feel out" the audience first, with formally directed songs, prayer, readings, and so on; then, by a friendly and confidence-engendering approach, gradually awaken a response among the people.

- Do not forget that the audience may also be feeling you out, so you should make a conscious effort to bid for their goodwill.

"Variety's the very spice of life, that gives it all its flavour" (William Cowper). And Aesop declared, "Familiarity breeds contempt."

- Why do you introduce a certain ploy? Are you copying someone else? Has it become merely a part of your weekly routine? What are you hoping to achieve? Do you actually fulfil that purpose?

- More than 2000 years ago Publilius Syrus recorded the maxim, "No pleasure endures if it is not seasoned by variety".

Samuel Johnson had the same idea: "*The joy of life is variety.*" So avoid monotony, think creatively. The Holy Spirit knows a thousand ways to keep the worship experience of the people freshly vital.

Why is it that in so many meetings only the women are asked to sing as a group, never the men, nor any other group within the audience?

Do the (usually) male leaders have a guilt complex about the limited role the ladies are often restricted to in the church? Is it a candle thrown to the feminine demand for a place in the sun? Perhaps the leader is moved by a doubtful assumption that women sing better than men? In the main, it shows that the leader is acting by habit, a mere reflex action, and that he has not made any serious attempt to plan his programme - so he does whatever first comes to mind; he takes the path of least effort.

You have no right to bully people into co-operating with you

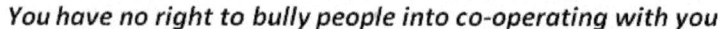

Chapter Thirteen

MUSIC TECHNIQUE

Martin Luther declared -

> "I am strongly persuaded that, after theology, there is no art that can be placed on a level with music; for besides theology, music is the only art capable of affording peace and joy to the heart like that induced by the study of the science of divinity. A proof of this is that the devil ... flees before the sound of music almost as much as before the word of God."[98]

The "Jesus '79" charismatic conference in Sydney, Australia, attracted attendances of more than 15,000 to its evening rallies. One of the features of those meetings was the great choir directed by Dr. Jesse Peterson, who also conducted a series of seminars on Christian music. He said -

> "When the Lord came to Moses and told him he was about to die, he also told him to prepare a message for the people. I can imagine Moses sitting down and thinking to himself, 'This is a tough assignment. I've got to give them everything at one time. How am I going to get this message across to the people in a way they will remember?' So what did he do? He wrote a song and taught it to the people (Deuteronomy 31:28-30; 32:1-44)."

---

[98] Quoted in Martin Luther, by Leonard W. Covie; published by Frederick A. Praeger, New York, 1969; pg 92-93.

Dr Peterson continued -

> "Moses recognised the significance of communicating through music. He understood the fact that music could preach the word as well as, if not better than, verbal preaching ... A very perceptive person taking notes may retain up to 15% of what he hears. But if you learn a song it will be with you forever. Most of us can still remember the nursery rhymes we learned as children.
>
> "There is an emotional and spiritual expression through music that is unequalled in any other form of communication. The world has learned the importance of this but it still has not been fully discovered by the church. In supermarkets music is played to settle people down and stop them running around frantically, thus giving them time to buy leisurely much more than they had first planned! There is another kind of music which has great therapeutic value when it is played for mentally retarded children.
>
> "Christians must recognise that the primary purpose of church music is not entertainment, but communication. Music that does not communicate has a limited value in church. Thus Christian music differs from secular music, which is often performed simply for its musical and aesthetic value."[99]

But if music is to be a tool for communication then it must speak the language of the people with whom you are trying to communicate. Many Christian musicians have failed to discern the different levels of musical appreciation attained by their audiences. They have played various kinds of modern or traditional music just because they happen to like those styles themselves, or because they think the people ought to like them.

---

[99] Note that the reference here is not to a difference in the nature or quality of the two kinds of music, but to the reasons for their performance, and the manner in which they are performed. The above comments were adapted from a tape-recording of one of Dr. Peterson's seminars.

But it defeats the purpose of worship to use music styles that seem to a given audience to be indecipherable, or shallow, or obsolete, or worldly, and the like.

The next chapter will explore in more depth the matter of music in the church and the form it should take. For the present, it is enough to mark the two points raised thus far:

- ♦ the immense importance of music in worship; and
- ♦ the necessity of using a music style that effectively communicates with the people.

Once those two things are established you can then give attention to technique.

Do not be over exuberant when you are song leading

Music is a fine servant but a false master.

- ♦ Worship is destroyed if it is dominated by the music, or by the musicians.

In some churches the musical tradition is so strong, everything else in the service is controlled by it and must conform to it; it has become impossible for worship to break free from the confining shape imposed by a rigid musical style. But music should be a servant of worship, not a master over it; it should assist the people, not control them.

- ♦ When used properly, music becomes a powerful tool of communication, a means of beautiful spiritual release.

Music can achieve those goals if it is kept subservient to the higher aims of worship, under the lordship of Christ and the direction of the Holy Spirit.

Contrary to popular opinion, music is essentially masculine.

- ♦ On the concert platform or in the church, successful musical performance requires a "masculine" approach.

I do not mean that a female performer must become "manly" before she can succeed, but only that she must have a quality of firmness, of strength, and authority.

- ♦ The same applies to a worship leader, whether man or woman. An effeminate approach to platform ministry (whether in voice, manner, or behaviour) will probably be ineffective - in a man, it may even be repulsive.

- ♦ This rule is always true in larger meetings, especially true in mixed meetings, and to some extent true even when women only are present.

The people will respond to, or react against, the character, mood, and behaviour of the leader.

- ♦ Display verve, vitality, good health, but not to excess. You should always convey a sense of inner control, of power under restraint, of disciplined energy, of definite purpose in your words and actions.

- Don't swamp the people with words, or drown them in an outpouring of uncontrolled emotion, or unsettle them by displaying a lack of personal discipline.

Some worship leaders become so caught up in the joy of the Lord, they abandon themselves to excitement, pouring out exhortations, ejaculations of praise, and a torrent of songs in a kind of wild exuberance. People become uneasy when their worship leader appears to have lost control of his own spirit. They will probably raise a protective barrier against such an emotional assault. They will unconsciously resist the leadership of that person, fearing that if they fully yield to his commands they too will be drawn into the fenceless desert of disorderly conduct. Zeal for Christ must be held within the bounds of discretion. Excitement must be tempered by wisdom. On the platform, holy joy and hot spiritual passion must not be allowed to collapse into unholy wildfire.

Give thought to the way you move on the platform. Do your movements enhance or hinder your ministry?

- Be graceful and pleasant in movement; especially avoid being jumpy, pacing nervously to and fro, fidgetting with papers or with the corner of the pulpit, and so on.
- The people prefer you to be neither a statue nor an acrobat, especially when you are leading congregational singing.

You do not have to be a good singer, but you MUST give attention to your speaking voice.

People don't want their worship leader to be a statue.

- Strive to speak clearly, directly, and with as low a pitch as you can readily manage, because a raspy or high-pitched voice tends to create tension in the audience, while a low round tone induces confidence.
- Most people unconsciously pitch their voices higher than usual when they face a crowd; watch carefully against that fault.

Once you begin speaking at a certain pitch in a public meeting it is difficult to change that pitch without hard conscious effort. If you discover you have pitched your voice too high, stop speaking as soon as you can, pause for a second or two, then deliberately lower your pitch as you begin to speak again. It is easier to begin with a low pitch; you will then have access to the full tonal range of your voice during the remainder of the meeting.

- ♦ Your voice is the foremost part of your ministry. Until you speak you remain largely colourless, unknown, without identity or personality.

Try then to speak in such a way as to achieve the maximum effect. Give strong attention to this! Listen to yourself. Cultivate clear enunciation. If you hear yourself slurring words, phrases, or sentences, practise speaking more clearly. So speak that every person can hear without effort every word you speak.

- ♦ If you do a lot of platform ministry (whether preaching or worship leading), treat your voice seriously.

People do not want their music leader to be a statue

I know too many preachers who have ruined their voices by careless use. Some of them have contracted an ulcerated larynx; polyps have grown in the throats of others. Some have lost their voices altogether; others have been vocally crippled for the rest of their lives. All of this was unnecessary. With moderate care and a little more knowledge, those preachers would not have suffered such miseries. Books are available on proper voice production. If you have never had any instructions in this area, I strongly recommend that you study one of these books, or that you at least take a few lessons from a speech therapist or a singing instructor.

Monotony of tone and phrase is a mortal enemy of good worship leading.

- ♦ Cultivate variety of expression, and prevent yourself from becoming one of those leaders who numb the minds of the people by constantly using the same trite phrases, the same banal idioms.

What tedium they produce! Such speech is called "hackneyed" because it is as mindless as the work performed by a common hack, a horse hired out for dull, drudging labour. It has the same wearying effect on the soul! So determine to say things differently. Think up new ways of expressing familiar ideas. Force yourself to smash the speech habits and routines that we are all prone to fall into. Listen to yourself as you speak. Appoint a trusted friend to act as your critic. If you discover that you have become like a broken record, mouthing the same phrases over and over again, escape that groove whatever it costs!

- ♦ Cultivate variety of tone, and away with that soporific monotone.

Practice speaking and reading aloud, using this formula: softer, louder, faster, slower, higher, lower. You will gain two benefits if you apply that formula to your speech: it will bring colour and life into your words; it will help you to avoid damaging your voice. (The people who get polyps and ulcers in their throats are not always those who use their voices vigorously, but may often be those who have spoken mostly in a monotone.)

Try reading the Psalms aloud, applying the above formula with great exaggeration; that is, read very loudly, then very softly, and so on. Keep practising until you have developed skill in using the full range of vocal modulation, then deliberately use that full range when you step onto the platform.

(Note: If you speak normally at the pulpit, as if you were conversing in your home, you will actually seem less than normal. In order to sound "natural" some exaggeration of style is needed. The degree of exaggeration will depend upon the size of your audience, the mood of the meeting, the message you are conveying, and so on.)

- Avoid, as you would a viper, personal speech mannerisms, such as peculiar inflections of the voice, oddly stressed syllables, adding syllables ("in the name of Christ-ah"), constant repetition of such phrases as "you know ... are you listening ... say `Amen'; or any other similar eccentricity.

There is also an inflated "professional" tone of voice that many people assume when they speak to a crowd, or lead the people in prayer. Perhaps this affected style arises from an unconscious desire to sound majestic or dramatic, or to convey an impression that they are being impelled by the power of the Holy Spirit. They merely sound pompous, even ridiculous.

Once again, listen to yourself as you speak. Check on yourself from time to time. Even the best of speakers can lapse into dreary speech habits and not be aware of it. Some other examples: *Praise the Lord! ... Hallelujah! ... Dear Jesus!* Some people can hardly say six words without interjecting one or more of their habitual phrases. I remember hearing a woman offering a public prayer in which every two or three words were punctuated by the expression Father God!"

The Golden Rule for worship leaders is, "Pay attention to your audience."

- Speak to be heard by the back row, not the front row; do this consciously and deliberately; and if they obviously did not hear, then repeat yourself.

- Look the people in the eye; it is most disconcerting to sit under a leader or preacher whose eyes wander all over the walls and the ceiling, but who never looks directly at the people.

It is important to maintain eye contact (unless, of course, you are facing a very large crowd).

- Do not focus attention on only one section of the audience, but make sure you regularly face each section as the meeting progresses.

If this requires you to turn sideways, or to move to one side of the platform, then move decisively and give that part of the audience your full attention for some time before turning back again. Do not swing back and forth. Do not keep moving around with little nervous steps. Avoid ALL nervous movements, twitchings, fiddlings, gestures, and mannerisms. When you move, move broadly, and with purpose.

The secret of success in worship leading is an ability to bring the people from a formal to an informal relationship with each other.

- Yet instead of seeing an audience brought from coldness and separation to warmth and friendship it is not uncommon to see the opposite achieved.
- The people want you to be more than a walking notice board or a human metronome.

They cannot be inspired by a log. A bulletin sheet and a machine would suffice merely to give announcements and stiffly keep time. Your audience expects to find, and will respond to, personality and colour in their worship leader. But they do not expect to be confronted by a clown. Strive to function at just that level of verve and informality necessary to relax the people and draw them together in love and hearty worship.

Chapter Fourteen

SONG TECHNIQUE

HANDLING THE SONG SERVICE

One of the best ways to facilitate rich worship is by a careful blending of songs and music.

- ♦ It is a mistake to begin a service with a song that is too high or too low pitched, has difficult rhythm or an unfamiliar tune, or is too fast or too slow; so begin with a well-known song, of middle pitch, easy rhythm, and easy to sing.

- ♦ A wise selection of songs can prepare the people either for deep, reflective worship, or for joyful praise, or for a message of rebuke, and so on.

For example, if your goal is to prepare them for a challenging message, and you want them to be ready to respond with enthusiasm, then begin with an easy song, mix in an occasional slower song, and gradually work toward faster, more difficult, more rousing songs, until you reach a climax with a specially chosen song just before the sermon. But beware of reaching the climax too soon, or of pressing for too high a climax, so that your last two or three songs, and perhaps even the sermon itself, become an anti-climax.

- ♦ If a song is pitched too high or too low, do not hesitate to ask for an alteration in the key.

If the musicians cannot do this, do not embarrass them, but change to another song. It is foolish to keep the people struggling to sing a difficult song.

- ♦ Sometimes a given congregation will sing a particular song very well, yet at the next meeting perform it poorly.

This is determined by the mood of the crowd, the songs that have gone before, the way the Holy Spirit may be influencing the service, and so on. Ordinarily you will find, if a song was highly successful last week, but a failure this week, that the people were not so well prepared this week for the special effort required by that song. They won't make the effort just because you want them to; they have to be emotionally and spiritually prepared for it.

- If you want to sing a song that contains some very high notes, then work up to it by selecting a couple of earlier songs that get close to the top notes you want the people to reach.

The same kind of preparation should be planned for any particularly demanding song.

- If a song is unknown, or the audience is plainly not yet in the mood to learn a new song, then drop it, choose another, and remain always adaptable to changes, both in the mood of the crowd and in the circumstances.

Rhythm is achieved, not by speed, but by the regular recurrence of a musical stress, whether that comes quickly or slowly.

- A song can have "beat" without having to be fast-moving.

A slow song can have just as much rhythm as a fast one. Resist the temptation continually to "speed up" the singing; if you don't, you will mainly succeed in wearying the people.

- Within the limits of the purpose set for the meeting, vary your choice of songs as much as possible.

You should mix the songs: slow and fast; with and without a "beat"; high-pitched and low-pitched; waltzes and marches; old and new; easy and difficult; and so on. The service will lose impact if all of the songs are of the same kind and are sung at the same speed.

- After a difficult or demanding song, give the people a rest, either by an easy, gentle song, or by a Bible reading, or a presented item, or a prayer, or some other device.

- Some songs are nearly impossible for the people to sing properly when they are seated, so arrange the programme so that difficult or demanding songs are sung when the audience is standing.

Successful song leading should turn coldness into warmth.

People usually dislike a song service being interrupted too frequently or for too long by interjected remarks.

While appropriate comments may be made about each song, both before and after it is sung, avoid preaching a series of sermonettes; do not preempt the preacher's role - the people came to hear him, not you.

Yet you should certainly do more than merely announce the next song. By wise and careful comments you can unite all of the disparate parts of the programme into one act of unified worship.

THE MUSICIANS

David Chislett, a friend of mine, wrote this -

> "Some Christians view the Old Testament teaching on instruments in worship as having no relevance for the Christian church. They only permit unaccompanied singing. "For example, in the 19th century the great Baptist preacher C.H. Spurgeon said that he would like to fill all the organ pipes in England with concrete. But most Christians have looked at the Old Testament as offering a pattern for church worship, particularly in the use of instruments."

Here are some guidelines about the musicians -

In the church the musicians should be treated neither as princes nor as peasants, but as priests.

- There have been two extremes: the musician given star billing and made into a hero; the musician made into a serf and given the lowest priority. Both are wrong.

Jesse Peterson says –

> There is no place for hero-worship in the kingdom of God - it is the very worst thing an audience can participate in or a musician encourage. But neither should music be relegated just to preliminaries, the warm-up before the 'real ministry' begins, the preaching of the word."

- There is a need in many places for pastors and musicians to have a greater awareness of, and respect for, each others' roles.

The pastors need to encourage the musicians to develop their gifts fully and should create opportunities for those gifts to be richly employed for the glory of God and the benefit of the church. On the other hand, as Asaph of old submitted to the authority of David, so musicians in the church must be yielded to the leadership of their pastor(s) (1 Chronicles 16:4-7).

- ♦ Musicians should be appointed in the church, not merely because they are skilled, but because they are called.

They are "ministers" of music, and ministry is a God-given thing, not to be assumed by human will alone. For this reason, musicians and vocalists should be discouraged from "drifting" in and out of the orchestra or choir. They should be specifically appointed to their task and enjoined to fulfil it in the fear of God.

- ♦ The leaders of the church should make sure that the musicians understand exactly what is expected from them, and that they know the boundaries of their responsibility and authority.

Keyboard pyrotechnics are out of place when the people are singing or worshipping.

There is no doubt a proper time for someone who is musically gifted to perform before the Lord to the best of his ability. His virtuosity may then become an act of worship in which the whole congregation can participate. But when the people are worshipping God in praise or song, the musicians should maintain a supportive not a dominant role.

You should prevent any of them from distracting the worship by displays of bravura, what Keith Ewing calls "demonstrations of keyboard artistry that are more sound than sense." I have seen a happily worshipping congregation subdued and then routed by over-zealous and too-clever musicians.

An audience will lose interest in singing if too much effort is required to rise above the music.

- ♦ Do not allow the musicians to play so loudly that the people are overwhelmed by sound; the music volume should be just enough to give a strong lead, but not so great as to discourage the people.

A congregation likes to enter into a friendly (although unconscious) competition with the musicians, to sing louder than they are playing. If that becomes impossible, the people will lose heart. I have been in some services where I could hardly hear my own voice, so I simply stopped singing.

♦ A proper blending of voice and music can create a beautiful spiritual unity and attract the mighty blessing of God (2 Chronicles 5:11-14; Psalm 133:1-3).

Don't let the musicians crush the people with sound.

Establish the fact that you are the worship leader, and that you will not surrender your role either to the congregation or to the musicians.

- It is YOUR task to set the pace, rhythm, and volume of the songs; do not surrender your rights to the musicians.
- If you cannot secure the co-operation of the orchestra you might as well not be on the platform.
- But remember also: no musician can co-operate with you unless he can see you without having to twist and turn.
- Nor can you expect the musicians to yield to your authority if you are unskilled and unsure of yourself, hence unable to give them the kind of clear directions they will need.

BEATING TIME

There are many church services, of course, where actual musical conducting of the singing is either not possible or not desirable - perhaps because of liturgical strictures, or for some other reason. But where it is possible for you to control the singing by an effective beating technique you should certainly do so. The notes that follow are general suggestions only. You will need to modify them to suit your own environment and style.

If you want to lead the singing, and not be led by it, then you must have a beat pattern that is clear, consistent, and commanding.

- The beating of many song leaders is mere show. They are not guiding the singing, but are simply waving their hands in time with the musicians.
- The purpose of beating is: first, to set the rhythm and pace of a song; second, to convey emotion and feeling; third, to indicate points where you want the people to hold a note, or to sing softly or loudly.

BEATING TECHNIQUE

Here are some practical pointers toward an effective beating technique.

- Your forearm and hand should move as a unit; avoid a flapping wrist; your arm should be firm, but not stiff; keep your motions generous and free, not cramped; cultivate the ability to use both arms, either singly or together.

- When using both hands, do not let them cross in front of your body, but rather let them meet in the centre; do not drop your hands below your waist, except perhaps on a strongly accented down-beat, or a cutting-off gesture.

- On the down-beat, face your palm downward; on the up-beat, face your palm upward; avoid a clenched fist; let your fingers be slightly apart with the palm slightly cupped.

- The accent should invariable come on a down-beat; not that every accent must have a down-beat, but every down-beat must be on an accent.

- Develop a decisive movement (usually a downward sweep) to close each song or verse.

- Avoid holding a song book while leading the singing.

- A slightly crouched posture, a shortened beat, will convey an impression of softness; by contrast, an open, extended posture, and a vigorous, wide beat, will lift the volume.

- Avoid facing an open palm toward the people, unless you want them to stop singing; an open palm has a repelling effect.

BEAT PATTERNS

Whatever hand movements you develop, make sure they convey to the musicians and to the people exactly what you want them to do. A good pattern will ensure that your hands are in the right place at the right time (e.g., raised high in readiness for an emphasised down-beat; or down low in readiness to lift the people to a crescendo).

> *"This then is how you should behave, dear friends. When you come together, each one of you should come with something to give: one will have a hymn, another a teaching, or a revelation, a tongue, or an interpretation. Just make sure that everything helps to build up the church. ... And follow this rule too: do everything with grace and dignity, and in an orderly manner." (1 Co 14:26,40).*

Make sure the musicians can see you easily

My lute awake, perform the last

by Sir Thomas Wyatt

My lute awake, perform the last
Labour, that thou and I shall waste,
And end that I have now begun:
And when this song is sung and past,
My lute! be still, for I have done.

As to be heard where ear is none;
As lead to grave in marble stone;
My song may pierce her heart as soon.
Should we then sigh, or sing, or moan?
No, no, my lute! for I have done.

The rocks do not so cruelly
Repulse the waves continually,
As she my suit and affection:
So that I am past remedy;
Whereby 2 my lute and I have done.

Proud of the spoil that thou hast got
Of simple hearts through Love's shot,
By whom, unkind, thou hast them won:
Think not he hath his bow forgot,
Although my lute and I have done.

Vengeance shall fall on thy disdain,
That makest but game on earnest pain;
Think not alone under the sun
Unquit 3 to cause thy lovers plain;
Although my lute and I have done.

May chance thee 4 lie withered and old
The winter nights, that are so cold,
Plaining in vain unto the moon;
Thy wishes then dare not be told:
Care then who list, for I have done.

And then may chance thee to repent
The time that thou hast lost and spent,
To cause thy lovers sigh and swoon:
Then shalt thou know beauty but lent,
And wish and want as I have done.

Now cease, my lute! this is the last
Labour, that thou and I shall waste;
And ended is that we begun:
Now is this song both sung and past;
My lute! be still, for I have done.

BIBLIOGRAPHY

Adventures of Huckleberry Finn, The; Mark Twain (1884).

Babylonian hymns and prayers; by David W Myhrman; *www.worldcat.org/title/**babylonian-hymns**-and-prayers.*

Believer's Bible Commentary; William Macdonald; Thomas Nelson Publishers; 1989.

Best Loved Poems of the American People, The; Selected by Hazel Felleman; Doubleday & Co. Inc., New York, 1936.

Bible Background Commentary; Intervarsity Press; Nottingham, UK; 1993.

Bible Knowledge Commentary, The; by John Walvoord and Roy Zuck; Cook Communications; Colorado Springs, Colorado, 1989.

Buried History; art. by G. G. Garner; March 1973.

Calvin's Commentaries; John Calvin (1509-1564).

Canterbury Tales; Geoffrey Chaucer; 1387.

Children's Encyclopedia; ed. Arthur Mee; Educational Book Society; London, 1963.

Christian Life, The; by John Calvin; ed. by J. H. Leith; Harper & Row; New York, 1984.

Christianity Today; art. by B. H. Leafblad; May 19th 1978.

College Press NIV Commentary, The; Joplin, Missouri; 1996.

Commentary on Ephesians, A; Charles Hodge (1797-1878).

Commentary on the Bible; Adam Clarke (1715-1832).

Commentary On The Old And New Testaments, A; John Trapp (1601-1669).

Commentary on the Old and New Testaments, A; Robert Jamieson, A. R. Fausset, David Brown; 1871.

Complete English Poems, The; John Donne; ed. by A. J. Smith; Penguin Books; 1982 reprint.

Complete Plain Words, The; by Ernest Gowers; 1954.

Dolly Dialogues, The; Anthony Hope (1894)

Explanatory Notes on the Whole Bible; John Wesley (1703-1791).

Exposition of the Entire Bible; John Gill (1690-1771).

Expositor's Bible Commentary, The; ed. Frank E. Gaebelein; Zondervan Publishers; Grand Rapids, Michigan.

Expository Commentary; H.A. Ironside (1876-1951).

Highwayman, The; by Alfred Noyes; Lothrop, Lee & Shepard Books; 1983.

Holman New Testament Commentary; ed. Max Anders; B & H Publishing Group; Nashville, Tennessee, 2004.

Iliad, The; tr. by E. V. Rieu; Penguin Books; 1957 reprint.

Institutes of the Christian Religion; Calvin; ed. by J. T. McNeill; tr. by Ford Battles; Westminster Press, Philadelphia.

Interpreter's Bible, The; Abingdon Press, New York, 1952.

IVP New Testament Commentary Series, The; Intervarsity Press; Nottingham, UK.

Jewish New Testament Commentary; David H. Stern; Jewish New Testament Publications, Inc., Clarksville, Maryland, 1982.

Matthew Henry's Commentary; Marshall, Morgan, and Scott; London, 1953.

Matthew Poole's Commentary; 1685.

Nelson's New Illustrated Bible Commentary; Thomas Nelson Inc., New York, 1999.

New Testament Commentary; Baker's Publishing House; Grand Rapids, Michigan, 1987.

Nicene and Post-Nicene Fathers, The; First Series, by W. B. Eerdmans Publishing Company; 1978 reprint.

Notes on the Bible; Albert Barnes (1798-1870).

Pageant of English Poetry, The; Oxford University Press; London, 1914.

People's New Testament Commentary, The; B. W. Johnson; Word Search Corporation; Nashville, Tennessee; 2010.

People's New Testament, The; by B. W. Johnson; 1891.

Poems of Alexander Pope, The; ed. By John Butt; Routledge; London, New York, 1963.

Poems of Robert Browning, The; Heritage Press; Norwalk, Ct., 1971.

Poor Man's Commentary On The Whole Bible, The; Robert Hawker; 1850.

Preacher's Commentary, The; Word Inc., Nashville, Tennessee, 1992.

Preacher's Outline and Sermon Bible; Word Search Corporation; Nashville, Tennessee, 2010.

Pulpit Commentary, The; ed. Joseph S. Exell, Henry Donald Maurice Spence-Jones, 1881.

Ruba'iyat of Omar Khayyam, The; Peter Avery & John Heath-Stubbs; Penguin Classics; London, 1983.

Shakespeare's Sonnets; The Folio Society Ltd., 1989.

Silver Poets of the Sixteenth Century; ed. Gerald Bullett; J. M. Dent & Sons Ltd. London.

Sir Thomas Browne, The Major Works; ed. C. A. Patrides; Penguin Books; London, 1977.

Tyndale Old Testament Commentary; Tyndale Press; 1969.

Tyndale Old Testament Commentary; Psalms 1-72; by Derek Kidner; Inter-Varsity Press; London, 1973.

Vincent's Word Studies; Marvin R. Vincent; 1886

What Luther Says; Compiled by Ewald M Plass; Concordia Publishing House; Missouri, 1959.

Wiersbe's Expository Outlines; Warren W. Wiersbe; Publisher, David C. Cook; Colorado Springs, Colorado.

Word Pictures In The New Testament; A. T. Robertson; 1933.

Printed in the USA
CPSIA information can be obtained
at www.ICGtesting.com
LVHW022320240924
791983LV00014B/453